D0407894

why?

why?

CHARLES TILLY

PRINCETON UNIVERSITY PRESS

PRINCETON AND OXFORD

Copyright © 2006 by Princeton University Press

Published by Princeton University Press, 41 William Street,
Princeton, New Jersey 08540
In the United Kingdom: Princeton University Press, 3 Market Place,
Woodstock, Oxfordshire OX20 1SY

All Rights Reserved

Library of Congress Cataloging-in-Publication Data

Tilly, Charles.Why? / Charles Tilly.
p.   cm.
Includes bibliographical references and index.
ISBN-13: 978-0-691-12521-3 (hardcover : alk. paper)
ISBN-10: 0-691-12521-X (hardcover : alk. paper)
1. Attribution (Social psychology) 2. Explanation. 3. Causation.
4. Reasoning (Psychology) I. Title.
HM1076.T55   2006
302'.12—dc22   2005024363

British Library Cataloging-in-Publication Data is available

This book has been composed in Janson Text and Horatio Lt. Std. Display

Printed on acid-free paper. ∞

pup.princeton.edu

Printed in the United States of America

10   9   8   7   6   5   4   3   2

To my surviving siblings
and their life companions:
Rich, Elisabeth, Carolyn, Reg,
Steve, and Elizabeth—
reasons enough

CONTENTS

PREFACE

Did you ever wonder why people give the reasons they do for what they have done, for what others have done to them, or more generally for what goes on in the world? I did, and ended up writing this book. Writing the book drove me off my usual course of analyzing large-scale political processes such as revolutions and democratization. Two different winds blew me off course.

First, noticing how mass media, students, and my fellow social scientists customarily explained complex social phenomena made me wonder why they focused so regularly on the decision making of a few influential actors while neglecting unanticipated consequences, incremental effects, and the incessant, subtle negotiation of social interaction. Both personal experience and professional studies of social processes, after all, had led me to think that people rarely accomplish exactly what they consciously plan, and constantly find events unrolling differently from what they anticipated. Why, then, do people's descriptions and explanations of social processes overwhelmingly emphasize conscious deliberation?

Second, my own plaintive claim that most social processes more often resemble intense conversation than, say, soliloquies or a grand master's planning of chess moves somehow rarely persuaded anyone. Maybe that was because my own analyses dealt with too large a social scale. Or maybe it was because I hadn't thought hard enough about what it usually takes to make a description or explanation comprehensible and credible. For better or for worse, I decided to address the double challenge at book length. Here is the result.

I don't for a moment claim to have discovered that reason giving is a social activity, and that valid reasons therefore vary from one social situation to another. In the book, I draw explicitly on Aristotle's ideas concerning poetics and rhetoric. If this were an academic treatise, I would surely also trace my line of argument back through American pragmatism via John Dewey and George Herbert Mead. In that lineage, the influential critic-philosopher Kenneth Burke insisted that words for motives actually describe situations, not inward states. Whimsically, Burke suggested that the claim even applied to dogs: "A sleek young terrier in the country has a vocabulary of motives considerably different from that of a fat, coddled, overfed poodle in the city, whose only adventures are confined to candy and a constitutional on hard pavements" (Burke 1989: 127). Different sorts of dogs acted out different reasons depending on their situations.

In a famous essay, sociologist C. Wright Mills picked up Burke's idea of a "vocabulary of motives," spelled out its social side, and explicitly identified his own formulation with those of John Dewey. In much more stilted language than he used in his hard-hitting and widely read critiques of American life and governmental policy, Mills argued that

The generic situation in which imputation and avowal of motives arise, involves, first, the *social* conduct of the (stated) programs of languaged creatures, *i.e.* programs and actions oriented with reference to the actions and talk of others; second, the avowal and imputation of motives is concomitant with the speech form known as the "question." Situations back of questions typically involve *alternative* or *unexpected* programs or actions of which phases analytically denote "crises." The question is distinguished in that it usually elicits another *verbal* action, not a motor response. The question is an element in *conversation*. (Mills 1963: 440)

In this congested passage and later in the same essay, Mills came close to equating avowal and attribution of motives to the giving of reasons, and to saying that they always accomplish the social work of justification, rationalization, and repair.

Aside from harking back to Aristotle now and then, the book you have before you spends almost no words laying out detailed theories, tracing their genealogies, or marking my agreements or differences with other theorists. The chapter on conventions does, it is true, say something about how the perceptive sociologist Erving Goffman treated similar matters. I also cheat a bit by slipping citations of academic works, including my own, into the text when a difficult point arises. I slip in those citations to help students who want to follow up intriguing ideas and specialists who wonder where I got those ideas. But instead of showing how my arguments articulate with previous work on reason giving, I have concentrated here on helping readers understand how reasons figure in social situations they encounter all the time. The acid test of the book's value is not whether it improves on the existing literature, but rather whether people who have read it see their own and other people's answers to the question "Why?" more clearly, or at least differently, than before.

Along the way, Andrew Abbott, Aaron Cicourel, Lynn Eden, Mona El-Ghobashy, Jack Katz, Douglas Mitchell, Katherine Newman, David Rothman, Robert Courtney Smith, Laura Tilly, Viviana Zelizer, and two anonymous readers offered me indispensable criticism, information, advice, and encouragement. Tim Sullivan's enthusiasm for publishing the book buoyed my spirits through a tortuous review process. Jon Munk's copyediting adroitly combined a quick eye and a light hand. An early version of chapter 1 appeared as "Reasons Why," *Sociological Theory* 22 (2004), 445–455; material from that article reappears here with permission of the American Sociological Association.

why?

WHY GIVE REASONS?

The first observers simply tried to figure out what was happening. On the morning of September 11, 2001, at 8:19 AM, flight attendant Betty Ong called American Airlines' Southeastern Reservations Office in Cary, North Carolina. She phoned from American Flight 11, which had left Boston for Los Angeles at 8 AM. In North Carolina, Ong reached Nydia Gonzalez. Ong told Gonzalez that hijackers had taken over their flight, had stabbed two other flight attendants, had killed at least one passenger, and had sprayed her and others with a substance that made their eyes burn and gave them trouble breathing (9/11 Report 2004: 5).

At 8:27, Gonzalez relayed Ong's call to Craig Marquis, duty manager at American Airlines' operations center in Forth Worth, Texas. At about the same time, air traffic controllers reported that the flight had made a sharp turn south near Albany, New York. "'They're going to New York!' Mr. Marquis remembers shouting out. 'Call Newark and JFK and tell them to expect a hijacking,' he ordered, assuming the hijackers would land the plane. 'In my wildest dreams, I was not thinking the plane was going to run into a building,' Mr. Marquis says" (CBS News 2002: 47). Veteran duty manager Marquis reasonably mapped the hijacking of Flight 11 into vivid previous episodes during which captors had demanded money, asylum, or release of political prisoners. They had grabbed the plane, he supposed, to hold the aircraft, its crew, and its passengers hostage for concessions. At nearly the same time, Boston air traffic controllers were telling the Federal Aviation Administration's Command Center that hijackers had probably taken over the plane (Duenes et al. 2004: A16). Continuing her whispered chronicle of events aboard the aircraft, at 8:38 Betty Ong reported that the plane was descending. Her call was cut off abruptly at 8:44 (9/11 Report 2004: 6).

The hijackers of Flight 11 soon proved Craig Marquis's reasons wrong. Two minutes after Gonzalez lost phone contact with Betty Ong, chief inspector Kevin McCabe of the U.S. Customs Service was looking east from his office window in Elizabeth, New Jersey. "He was sipping coffee and talking on the phone at 8:46," he later reported to Steven Brill, "when he saw the first plane hit the World Trade Center. Because he had seen how big the plane was, he thought it might be an attack. He flipped on the television, then called the Customs office in New York, which was at the Trade Center, to find out what was going on" (Brill 2003: 1).

A few minutes after McCabe's call to headquarters, Bryant Gumbel was broadcasting for CBS News from Manhattan. He had just heard that an unidentified plane had crashed into the World Trade Center. At 8:52, his first eyewitness on the line was Stewart Nurick, who was waiting a table in a SoHo restaurant when "I literally saw a . . . it seemed to be a small plane. . . . I just heard a couple noises, it looked like it bounced off the building, and then I just saw a huge ball of fire on top of the building. And just lots of smoke and what looked to be debris or glass falling down" (CBS News 2002: 16). A moment later, Wendell Clyne, doorman at the Marriott World Trade Center Hotel, spoke to Gumbel:

> GUMBEL: Okay, so you were standing outside. Tell us what you saw and what you heard.
>
> CLYNE: I heard first an explosion. And I just figured that it was a plane passing by. Then all of sudden, stuff just started falling like bricks and paper and everything. And so I just kind of ran inside to get away from the falling debris and glass. Then when it kind of stopped, I heard a guy

screaming. Where I looked over, there was a guy that was on fire, so I ran over and I tried to put the fire out on him. And he was screaming. I just told him to roll, roll, and he said he couldn't. And then another guy came over . . . and put the flames out on him. (CBS News 2002: 17)

It was about two minutes past nine.

Gumbel switched to a third eyewitness, Theresa Renaud, who was watching the World Trade Center from her apartment at Eighth Avenue and Sixteenth Street, about two miles north of the Center. "Approximately ten minutes ago," reported Renaud,

there was a major explosion from about the 80th floor—looks like it's affected probably four to eight floors. Major flames are coming out of the north side and also the east side of the building. It was a very loud explosion, followed by flames, and it looks like the building is still on fire on the inside.

Oh, there's another one—another plane just hit. [gasps; yelling] Oh, my God! Another plane has just hit—it hit another building, flew right into the middle of it. My God, it's right in the middle of the building.

GUMBEL: This one into [Tower 2]?

RENAUD: Yes, yes, right in the middle of the building. . . . That was definitely . . . on purpose.

GUMBEL: Why do you say that was definitely on purpose?

RENAUD: Because it just flew straight into it. (CBS News 2002: 18)

Filmmaker Jules Naudet, who had been producing a documentary on a downtown Manhattan fire company, had gone to the scene with the battalion chief after the first plane crashed into the World Trade Center. He was filming firefighters' actions in the lobby of the North Tower, the first tower hit, when the second aircraft struck the other tower: "Suddenly we heard an explosion coming from outside, and as I turned to look out the windows, I saw flaming debris falling in the courtyard and then heard a radio call announcing that Tower 2 had been hit by another plane. Any thought that this was simply a terrible accident vanished: New York was under attack" (CBS News 2002: 23). Washington, D.C., was also under attack. A perplexing calamity had begun.

When commandeered commercial aircraft crashed into New York's World Trade Center, Washington's Pentagon, and a Pennsylvania field that September morning, people across the world began asking for reasons why. Why had someone perpetrated this vicious violence? Why had they targeted the United States? Why hadn't American authorities prevented the assault? Observers quickly shifted from simply making sense of what was happening to seeking reasons for the disaster. Direct participants faced the double challenge of finding reasons both for the terrible episode as a whole and for the specific incidents they had suffered, witnessed, or caused.

On the scene, emergency workers activated their routines without asking too many questions. Only as they worked did they start searching seriously for credible reasons for the disaster they were seeing. New York Fire Department Paramedic Gary Smiley, for example, was working overtime in downtown Brooklyn when the radio in his ambulance broadcast word that a plane had hit the 110-story North Tower (Tower 1) of the World Trade Center. The call had come at 8:48 AM. Within a few minutes, Smiley's crew rushed across the Brooklyn Bridge to Manhattan.

Smiley set up a triage area between the two towers. He was carrying an injured woman who had just left Tower 1 across the street when the woman started shouting "Plane." He looked up and saw the second aircraft hit the South Tower (Tower 2). It was 9:03 AM, just seventeen minutes after the first crash. Debris began falling on them, so partway across the street he pushed the woman to the ground and threw himself on top of her. A severed, burning human arm scorched his back. "It was chaos," he later reported. "Everyone was running around. Then it clicked in my head. I knew exactly what was going on. I was there in 1993 when they bombed the building. I ended up taking care of a hundred people across the street in the Millennium Hotel. So I knew this was an attack. That's what we started telling people, and that's what got them moving" (Fink and Mathias 2002: 33). Smiley first figured out his own reasons for what was happening, then told other people those reasons. By his account, people not only accepted his reasons, but also acted on them at once. He moved his ambulance to a safer location, evaded the falling bodies of people who were jumping to their deaths from the highest floors of the North Tower, and started into the tower for rescue operations. At that point (9:50 AM) the South Tower fell into flaming ruins.

Soon after the South Tower fell, Smiley was going to the rescue of other paramedics who were trapped in the tower's rubble. That work, however, ended fast. A rush of air from the sudden collapse (at 10:29 AM) of the North Tower picked Smiley up and slammed him to the pavement. He crawled under a truck, thinking he might die in the suffocating dust. Then, according to his recollections, he grew angry as he remembered how his father had died in a random street robbery three years earlier, and reflected on how his own death would hit his two children. Again a click:

> My mind just switched at that point, and I think that's really what gave me a desire to get out of there. Something just clicked, and I thought, I know I'm not going to die today. I'm going to get out of here.
>
> You know how people say, "God had other plans for you." I think it was my father who had other plans for me. He had to be looking out for me, and I just started digging. I don't know how long I was under the truck before I figured this out, but I started crawling my way out of there, digging through the rocks and the debris. Just as I got out, a

fireman who had also been lodged in the debris had gotten himself out. Both of us staggered around. (Fink and Mathias 2002: 34)

With all of his exposed skin burned, Smiley made it to a delicatessen on North End Avenue, where a number of injured police and fire-fighters had already sought refuge. There they heard explosions, and gave reasons for them: "One of the cops thought that it might be secondary explosions. When terrorists do this sort of thing, they'll put secondary bombs around to kill the rescue workers. That's an earmark of terrorism. And at that point you didn't know what to believe. Everybody had lost all concept of what was going on, and everything was up for grabs. For all we knew, they had attacked all of Manhattan" (Fink and Mathias 2002: 35). Still, by that time, many people on the spot were already sharing a definition of what was hap-pening and what to do about it: terrorists are attacking us, and we have to defend ourselves against them.

High officials also rushed to the disaster scene and sought reasons for what they found. New York City Police Commissioner Bernard Kerik had just finished exercising at his headquarters when aides pounded on his shower door to tell him that a plane had hit the top of the World Trade Center. Siren sounding and lights flashing, he and two of his men drove over close to the buildings, where they saw people leaping to their deaths from the North Tower. Kerik sent out orders for a citywide mobilization of police. Shortly thereafter, the second plane hit the South Tower, scattering aircraft fragments and body parts into the plaza below. (Since they couldn't see the aircraft, the commissioner's bodyguard Hector Santiago reported later, "The boss thinks it might have been a bomb. Now you think terrorist, and now he's getting into the groove" [Fink and Mathias 2002: 106].)

Running for their lives, Kerik and his aides barely escaped. They took shelter behind the post office at 7 World Trade Center. Then, remembered Kerik,

I looked back out. I saw the damage. At that point, I could hear aviation and the pilots yelling on the radio that it was a commercial airliner. I realized at that minute that we were under attack. I yelled to John [Picciano, his chief of staff] to get on the telephone to call headquarters, but there was no phone service. The cell phones were down, so we're calling on the radio. I'm yelling for them to get aviation to close down the airspace. We needed air support, and I'm screaming at these guys to get me air support.

They're looking at me, like "Is there a fucking number to call for an F-16?" Like "Who do we call? How do we do that?"

But aviation had taken care of that and closed down the airspace. They had called in the military. I ordered the entire city to be shut down at that point. All bridges and tunnels closed. No entry. No exit. My main concern at that point was that there could be other secondary attacks set up on the ground. They're hitting us from above, did they do anything on the ground? Are they on the ground? My other concern was who the hell they were. Who are they? You know, as all of these events were unfolding, you're trying to put it all together. You're trying to think of so many things at once. (Fink and Mathias 2002: 110–11)

Soon Mayor Rudolph Giuliani joined Kerik. The mayor called the White House, learning that another aircraft had hit the Pentagon and that (with President Bush in Florida) the presidential staff was evacuating the White House. The New York contingent set up a command center near what remained of the World Trade Center, only to be jolted by the South Tower's collapse. They moved their temporary headquarters to the city's police academy on East Twentieth Street. That day's performances gave Kerik and Giuliani national political visibility; it moved Kerik toward nomination as Secretary of the U.S. Department of Homeland Security in 2004.[1]

---

[1] Kerik withdrew himself from contention for the job after a few days, as reporters dug into his background and Kerik himself conceded that he had employed an illegal

What Reasons for This Book?

As eyewitnesses at the World Trade Center and Pentagon searched for reasons, they followed an extremely general human routine. We might even define human beings as reason-giving animals. While, by some definitions, other primates employ language, tools, and even culture, only humans start offering and demanding reasons while young, then continue through life looking for reasons why.

Reasons provide organized answers to the question "Why does (did, should) X do Y?" X can be you as you tell me why you arrived late for our rendezvous, me as I explain my winning of the lottery, or the hijackers who piloted aircraft into the World Trade Center and the Pentagon. X need not be a person or people; X can be God, evil spirits, Islam, communism, or just plain Them. X sometimes means individuals, groups, organizations, categories, forces, or invisible entities. X produces Y.

The World Trade Center disaster provoked reason giving at multiple levels, including:

- Why did the hijackers seize the aircraft and crash them into the towers?
- Why did the buildings burst into flames and collapse?
- (In the case of a participant) Why did I behave as I did? Why did *we* (whatever the we) behave as we did?
- (In the cases of participants and observers) why did other people (considered as individuals or as groups) behave as they did?
- What causes terrorism?
- What causes violence in general?

---

immigrant as housekeeper and nanny without filing tax reports on her. After another couple of weeks' brouhaha, Kerik also resigned from Giuliani's prosperous post–9/11 security consulting firm, saying that unfair allegations concerning the nanny, his love life, and past associations with criminals were hurting the firm. At least those were the reasons he gave: Lipton and Rashbaum 2004, Rashbaum and Dwyer 2004.

Moving among multiple levels, this book looks sympathetically but searchingly at reason giving. It asks how, why, and in what different ways people supply reasons for the things they do, that others do, that happen to them, or that happen to other people—not so much grand general reasons for life, evil, or human frailty as the concrete reasons that different sorts of people supply or accept as they go about their daily business, deal with hardship, pass judgment on each other, or face emergencies such as the 9/11 disaster.

The book you are starting to read focuses on the social side of reason giving: how people share, communicate, contest, and collectively modify accepted reasons rather than how individual nervous systems process new information as it comes in. It worries little about whether the reasons people give are right or wrong, good or bad, plausible or implausible. Instead, it concentrates on the social process of giving reasons. Nor does it spend much time on general intellectual discussions of why things occur as they do, much less on how to resolve broad disagreements about reasons for big events.

The attacks of 9/11 inspired plenty of debate. "There is no disputing," comment the editors of a volume concerning the implications of 9/11, "that the underlying significance of September 11 can only be comprehended when placed in its full context, yet the boundaries of that context are themselves hotly contested" (Hershberg and Moore 2002: 1). Seriously proposed reasons for 9/11, the editors go on to say, include al-Qaeda fanaticism, misguided American foreign policy, peculiar characteristics of Middle Eastern regimes, collapse of a previously stable (if dangerous) world order, and more. All those themes sound quite familiar to me. Most of my own professional work involves sorting out reasons for political processes at a broad scale: why revolutions occur, what causes democratization and dedemocratization, why terrorism takes its many forms, and so on. Instead of sorting out such broad political questions, however, this book concentrates on the social process of giving reasons at the person-to-person scale. Reason giving turns out to be momentous at this scale as well.

Giving of reasons, as we will soon see, connects people with each other even when observers might find the reasons flimsy, contrived, or fantastic. In uncertain situations such as the 9/11 attacks, most people first adapt reasons for what is happening from models they have already learned through interaction with other people. Available models vary dramatically from group to group, situation to situation, and relation to relation. Regardless of their content, however, reasons provide rationales for behaving one way or another and shared accounts of what is happening. They also make statements about relations between the people giving and receiving those reasons.

Look again at reason giving on 9/11 at the World Trade Center. At least emergency workers and city officials had previous experience, available categories, and established routines to draw on as they sought reasons for what was happening. People who worked in the towers generally had much less to go on. Even savvy Chuck Allen shifted his reasons as the disaster unfolded.

Allen ran computer operations at Lava Trading, on the 83rd floor of the North Tower. Allen was also a licensed pilot and a ham radio operator. When he saw a plane flying low south along the Hudson River about 8:45 AM, he was surprised, but supposed that it was approaching Newark Airport. A moment later, however, he noticed the familiar sound of a pilot gunning the aircraft's engine, then heard a roar as the plane hit the building thirteen floors above him. The building started shuddering, debris began falling, and fires fed by cascading airplane fuel broke out.

In answer to his computer programmer's frightened question over the intercom, Allen shouted, "A jet-helicopter hit the building, I think" (*Der Spiegel* 2001: 48). Later, as he and others clattered down stairways from the 83rd floor, he tried sending out Mayday signals on the two-way radio he carried with him:

> As soon as he had established contact he was thrown off the air: "All traffic has been cleared to keep frequencies clear for emergency calls. Get off the frequency." They thought he was playing around. From the bits of conversation he was able to gather that an American Airlines jet had hit the towers. He didn't get it. "Okay. Planes crash, let's face it. But why into the towers? The pilot had the whole Hudson River, for God's sake. What was wrong with this guy?" (*Der Spiegel* 2001: 55)

After Allen led a group down the stairs from the 83rd floor and exited into the plaza north of the building, a police officer told him "We believe this was intentional" (*Der Spiegel* 2001: 108). A new set of reasons was beginning to emerge.

Even as they fled the stricken buildings, survivors of the 9/11 attacks in New York began to think through reasons for the disaster. Gerry Gaeta worked as an architect for the Port Authority of New York, which managed the World Trade Center. As he later recounted his perilous descent from the North Tower's 88th floor (five floors above Chuck Allen's starting point), Gaeta told how he and a group from his office made their way through debris and darkness. The fire that resulted from the aircraft's impact had scorched Elaine Duch of the real estate department, laminating her dress to her skin.

> Elaine was one of the first to come down. She was with Doreen Smith, another secretary who worked in the real estate department. One of the girls who worked for [Larry] Silverstein [the building's incoming leaseholder] had wrapped a sweater around Elaine's waist to give her some decency. There was a big knot in the back tied with the arms of the sweater. Doreen went ahead of Elaine, clearing the way and ready to catch her if she should fall, and I walked behind her, holding on to

the knot so she would not fall. We walked 88 floors that way. When we got down to the 76th floor, the stairs led to a crossover corridor that was designed to create a smoke barrier. It was about 50 feet long and had a fire-rated door at each end to provide a smoke-proof enclosure. We went through the first door, but the second door wouldn't open. I kicked it a dozen times but it wouldn't budge. I started to think that maybe this was part of the terrorist plot—that they had calculated in their minds that people would be trying to escape, so they had locked the stairwell doors. In reality, I figured out later, the jolt of the plane hitting the building probably racked and jammed the door. (Murphy 2002: 52–53)

Gaeta first thought that terrorists had plotted the disaster down to the last detail. As a trained architect, however, he later complicated the story; he brought in unanticipated consequences of the crash.

At least as they later told their tales, many of the survivors that Dean Murphy, Mitchell Fink, Lois Mathias, and *Der Spiegel*'s reporters interviewed for their vivid books of 9/11 memoirs reported almost immediately coding the disaster they had experienced as a terrorist attack. Perhaps that was because American courts had already convicted Muslim militants for their 1993 attempt to bring down the World Trade Center with an explosive-packed van. Or maybe it was because the U.S. government, prompted by the bombing of the USS *Cole* in Yemen during 2000, was already warning Americans about Osama bin Laden's evil intentions well before 9/11 (State 2001a).

In any case, many survivors also likened the attack to the first low blow of a new war, another Pearl Harbor. Richard Brown, economist with the Federal Deposit Insurance Corporation, was attending a meeting of the National Association for Business Economics with his wife, Cathy, and two of their four children (aged seven and ten) at the World Trade Center's Marriott Hotel when American Airlines Flight 11 struck the adjacent North Tower. The Browns evacuated quickly. Richard Brown later reported: "After the planes had hit the buildings and we were waiting in Battery Park, I had told them it was like Pearl Harbor. They understand these things sometimes in terms of recent blockbuster movies. I told them it was like *Pearl Harbor* and *Titanic* combined" (Murphy 2002: 110). For interviewed survivors, at least, the reasons for their terrible experience did not seem far to seek. Terrorists had tried to do them in, and had almost succeeded.

On further reflection, survivors and witnesses often elaborated their stories. Kimberly Morales, a senior at nearby Borough of Manhattan Community College, for example, had second thoughts. From close to her school she saw the airplane crash, the explosion, the fire, and eventually the North Tower's collapse. She also saw desperate people jump from the building to their deaths. On her way back to the Bronx: "It was an emotional trip home. I thought a lot about politics. I was really mad and didn't know where to direct my anger. Where were the people in our government whose jobs were to prevent things like this? Were they off in their million-dollar yachts and fancy vacations while we were suffering through this?" (Murphy 2002: 128). The search for reasons led rapidly to assessments of responsibility and blame. Even if unnamed terrorists piloted their commandeered aircraft into the twin towers, the Pentagon, and a Pennsylvania field, someone else's dereliction had allowed them to seize the aircraft.

Public officials engaged in a similar search for reasons, responsibility, and blame. In the course of a widely praised press conference on September 11, New York's Mayor Giuliani placed the reasons in context: "I believe that the people in New York City can demonstrate our resolve and our support for all of the people that were viciously attacked today by going about their lives and showing everyone that vicious, cowardly terrorists can't stop us from being a free country and a place that functions. And we'll do everything we can to make that point" (Adler and Adler 2002: 9). The reasons—"vicious, cowardly terrorists" who sought to destroy the functioning of "a free country"—dictated the proper reaction, calm determination.

The same day, U.S. Secretary of State Colin Powell issued a similar first response to the attacks: "Once again we see terrorism; we see terrorists, people who don't believe in democracy, people who believe that with the destruction of buildings, with the murder of people, they can somehow achieve a political purpose. They can destroy buildings, they can kill people, and we will be saddened by this tragedy, but they will never be allowed to kill the spirit of democracy. They cannot destroy our society. They cannot destroy our belief in the democratic way" (State 2001b). The tragedy occurred, according to Secretary Powell, because terrorists with twisted minds thought—wrongly—that they could shake American resolve by destroying American public buildings. In his address to Congress nine days after the devastating attacks of 9/11, U.S. President George W. Bush elaborated on Powell's reasons by identifying the culprits and associating them with villains across the world. "Our war on terror," declared Bush, "begins with al-Qaida, but it does not end there. It will not end until every terrorist group of global reach has been found, stopped, and defeated" (State 2002: i).

Varieties of Reasons

Whether public officials, emergency workers, or community college students, people do not give themselves and others reasons because of some universal craving for truth or coherence. They often settle for reasons that are superficial, contradictory, dishonest, or—at least from an observer's viewpoint—farfetched. Whatever else they are doing when they give reasons, people are clearly negotiating their social lives. They are saying something about relations between themselves and those who hear their reasons. Giver and receiver are confirming, negotiating, or repairing their proper connection.

Commonly given reasons fall into four overlapping categories.

1. *Conventions:* conventionally accepted reasons for dereliction, deviation, distinction, or good fortune: my train was late, your turn finally came, she has breeding, he's just a lucky guy, and so on

2. *Stories:* explanatory narratives incorporating cause-effect accounts of unfamiliar phenomena or of exceptional events such as the 9/11 catastrophe, but also such as betrayal by a friend, winning a big prize, or meeting a high school classmate at Egypt's Pyramids twenty years after graduation

3. *Codes* governing actions such as legal judgments, religious penance, or awarding of medals

4. *Technical Accounts* of the outcomes in the first three: how a structural engineer, a dermatologist, or an orthopedic surgeon might explain what happened to Elaine Duch on the World Trade Center's 88th floor after a hijacked aircraft struck the building on 9/11

Each of the four ways of giving reasons has distinctive properties. Each of them varies in content depending on social relations between giver and receiver. Each of them, among other consequences, exerts effects on those social relations, confirming an existing relation, repairing that relation, claiming a new relation, or denying a relational claim. But the four sorts of reason giving differ significantly in form and content. Each can be valid in a way that the others cannot.

Conventions involve no pretense of providing adequate causal accounts. If I start explaining in detail why I spilled my coffee on your newspaper—how I had a bad night's sleep, have been worrying about my job, recently developed a tremor it is hard to control—you may well become impatient. "Oops, I'm such a klutz!" may suffice, especially if I offer to get you a fresh newspaper. ("Sorry, I tripped on the rug" might also do.) Conventions vary enormously according to the social circumstances; given an identical dereliction, deviation, or good fortune, for example, a reason that satisfies a seatmate on the bus will usually not placate one's spouse. Conventions claim, confirm, repair, or deny social relations. They therefore differ greatly depending on the social relations currently in play.

Exceptional events and unfamiliar phenomena, however, call up different reasons why; they call up *stories*. People experiencing an egregious failure, a signal victory, a spectacular faux pas, a shared tragedy, or mysterious sounds in the night do not settle for "It was just the breaks." They, too, try to match reasons to the circumstances and social relations at hand, but now the reasons take on weight. Similarly, major life transitions such as marriage, divorce, or the death of a parent call for weightier accounts than conventions provide. In general, reasons for exceptional events complement explanations with at least hints of justification or condemnation: the company gave me a bigger bonus than you because I worked harder and sold more computers. Implied claims concerning the quality, intensity, durability, and propriety of relations between givers and receivers far exceed the claims tied to conventions.

Stories matter greatly for social life because of three distinctive characteristics. First, they rework and simplify social processes so that the processes become available for the telling; X did Y to Z conveys a memorable image of what happened. Second, they include strong imputations of responsibility, and thus lend themselves to moral evaluations: I get the credit, he gets the blame, they did us dirt. This second feature makes stories enormously valuable for evaluation after the fact, and helps account for people's changing stories of events in which they behaved less than heroically. Third, stories belong to the relationships at hand, and therefore vary from one relationship to another; a television interviewer gets a different story of a lost football game from the one that players tell each other.

Further, stories truncate cause-effect connections. They typically call up a limited number of actors whose dispositions and actions cause everything that happens within a delimited time and space. The actors sometimes include supernatural beings and mysterious forces—for example, in witchcraft as an explanation of misfortune—but the actors' dispositions and actions explain what happened. As a consequence, stories inevitably minimize or ignore the causal roles of errors, unanticipated consequences, indirect effects, incremental effects, simultaneous effects, feedback effects, and environmental effects (Tilly 1995, 1996). They conform to dominant modes of storytelling. In fact, most of the early reason giving for 9/11 took the form of stories.

In contrast to stories, *codes* need not bear much explanatory weight so long as they conform to the available rules. (When I served the U.S. Navy as a rule-wielding supply and disbursing officer, veteran Chief Petty Officer Edward McGroarty, who helped train me on the job, used to joke, "There's no reason for it: it's just policy!") Religious prescriptions, law codes, and prestigious systems of honors overflow with reasons, but those reasons describe how what happened conforms to the code at hand rather than what actually caused the outcome. Third parties such as judges, priests, and awards committees figure extensively in the giving of reasons according to codes.

When we wanted to copy some crucial and voluminous nineteenth century household records from Milan, Louise Tilly and I had an instructive encounter with codes proposed by Ragionier [Accountant] Ciampan, director of Milan's municipal archives. First the Ragionier dismissed us by insisting that only the city's mayor could authorize outsiders to use the records. When we pulled strings and actually returned with a letter from the mayor, I asked the Ragionier when I could start setting up my camera. The small man strode to a huge book of municipal regulations on their stand by the window, opened to a passage declaring that "no one external to the archives may photograph their contents," placed his hand on the great book, raised his other hand in the air, and declared, "I am bound by the law." We painfully copied the records by hand.

Even victims of codes often accept them as judgments. David Patterson (whom we will meet again in chapter 3) suffered from the electronic industry's contraction in the mid-1980s. During the decade's early prosperous years, his firm had promoted him from an executive position in its California office to a division headship in the New York metropolitan area. He had moved his family, including two teenagers, into a prosperous New York suburb. The kids made painful adjustments to the move. Then, during the mid-1980s slump, the company closed his division, terminated him, and gave him four weeks' severance pay. He could not find another executive job. Despite that, he gave Katherine Newman a coded reason for his plight: "A policy is a policy and a procedure is a procedure. That's the way you operate. If you're part of the corporate world you understand. It doesn't make you feel better; it doesn't smooth anything, but that's the way you do it. You accept it . . . otherwise you can't work in that environment. . . . If I got back into the game, I'd play it the same way. And I would expect the same things to happen to me again" (Newman 1988: 77). Of course, all of us have cursed at stupid policies from time to time. But, for those who play the game, codes have an air of inevitability, even of sanctity.

Finally, *technical accounts* vary enormously with regard to internal structure and content, but they have in common the claim to identify reliable connections of cause and effect. As he reflected on his futile attempt to kick open a fireproof door on the World Trade Center's 76th floor, Gerry Gaeta supplemented his initial story about the terrorists' foresight with a cause-effect account based on his expertise as an architect. Structural engineers center their cause-effect connections in mechanical principles, physicians in the dynamics of organisms, and economists in market-driven processes. Although engineers, physicians, and economists sometimes spend great energy in justifying their expertise when under attack, earnestly demonstrating that they reached their conclusions by widely accepted professional procedures, on the whole they center their giving of reasons on putative causes and effects. Whole professions and organized bodies of professional knowledge stand behind them.

Roughly speaking, then, reasons why distribute this way:

	Popular	Specialized
Formulas	Conventions	Codes
Cause-Effect Accounts	Stories	Technical Accounts

From left to right, the diagram represents the extent to which ordered, disciplined, internally coherent schemes dominate reason giving, with "popular" reasons being widely accessible, and "specialized" reasons relying on extensive training in the discourse. Top to bottom, the diagram runs from X-to-Y matching, in which criteria of appropriateness rather than causality prevail (formulas), to tracing of causal processes from X to Y (cause-effect accounts). Obviously, the scheme orders claims made by givers and/or accepted by receivers rather than any judgment of their adequacy by third parties, including you and me.

All four kinds of reasons commonly do relational work. The most invisible work simply *confirms* the relation between giver and receiver, for example as a penitent accepts a priest's interpretation of her sins and the priest's prescription for proper recompense to man and God in a code that has little or nothing to do with causes and effects. More visibly, reason giving often *establishes* relations, as in the case of an interviewer who explains the purpose of a survey when calling to ask about preferences in food, television, or politics. It sometimes *negotiates* relations, as when the author of a technical account displays professional credentials to make a claim on a listener's respect and compliance. Finally, much reason giving *repairs* relations, as someone who has inflicted damage on someone else tells a story to show that the damage was inadvertent or unavoidable and therefore, despite appearances, does not reflect badly on the relationship between giver and receiver. The phrase "I'm sorry, but . . . " often starts a story that does relational repairs. Both formulas and cause-effect accounts do relational work.

Formulas identify an appropriate correspondence between Y (the event, action, or outcome at hand) and X (its antecedent), but enter little or not at all into the causal chain connecting Y to X. Cause-effect accounts trace causal lines from X to Y—even if we observers find those causal lines absurd or incomprehensible. "Popular" reasons obviously vary from one public to another, for example as a function of religiosity and religious creed. Specialized reasons likewise vary strikingly from discipline to discipline; theologians elaborate both codes and technical accounts that differ deeply from those proposed by medical practitioners.

Sophisticated readers should guard against an easy and erroneous pair of assumptions: that popular reasons peddle inferior, ignorant, and excessively simplified versions of codes and technical accounts, and that truly sophisticated people therefore never resort to conventions or stories. We sophisticates easily make the mistake because we frequently have to translate our own codes or technical accounts into terms that people who work in other idioms will understand. Russell Hardin makes a necessary distinction between knowledge that a "super-knower" might have available—for example, knowledge embedded in the theory of relativity—and the everyday knowledge of practical persons. He calls for an economic theory of knowledge based on street-level epistemology:

> An economic theory of knowledge is a theory of why the typical individual or even a particular individual comes to know various things. In an economic theory, it makes sense to say that you know one thing and I know a contrary thing in some context. I might eventually come to realize that my knowledge is mistaken and therefore correct it, especially after hearing your defense of your contrary knowledge. But there is no role for a super-knower who can judge the truth of our positions. We are our own judges. If we wish to seek better knowledge, it is we who must decide from what agency or source to seek it. Street-level epistemology is not about what counts as knowledge in, say, physics, but rather [about] your knowledge, my knowledge, the ordinary person's knowledge. (Hardin 2002: 4)

In everyday life, we all deploy practical knowledge. We draw practical knowledge not only from individual experience but also from the social settings in which we live. Practical knowledge ranges from logics of appropriateness (formulas) to credible explanations (cause-effect accounts). Appropriateness and credibility vary from one social setting to another.

Different pairs of givers and receivers therefore offer contrasting types of reasons for the same event. Consider 9/11. We have already seen witnesses and participants offering conventions ("this is war" and "this is terror") as well as stories ("terrorists deliberately crashed their planes"), and have received hints of technical accounts in Gerry Gaeta's explanation of how the crash jammed World Trade Center fire doors. Since that time, engineers and physicists have spent a great deal of time reconstructing how the impact of two aircraft (more importantly, as it turned out, the ignition of their fuel) brought down two buildings designed to withstand huge shocks; technical accounts of 9/11 have multiplied (see, for example, Glanz 2004). But so have coded analyses on the part of anti-American theologians and international lawyers for whom the attacks qualify as just deserts. Reasons do not vary so much by type of event as by type of conversation—who is speaking to whom makes a tremendous difference.

Of course, intermediate forms of reason giving exist. One form sometimes mutates into another as people interact. In religious communities, "God wills it" stands halfway between a convention and a story, having more or less explanatory power depending on prevailing beliefs about divine intervention in human affairs. The talk of baseball fans zigzags crazily among conventions, stories, codes, and technical accounts, leaving the follower of some other sport—or none—mystified by its leaps from detailed cause-effect reasoning to simple sloganeering. Professionals and teachers often shift between technical accounts and stories as they see that their listeners do or don't follow the lines of explanation that prevail in their fields. Long-term patients and hypochondriacs become expert in their diseases, engaging their physicians in semitechnical discussions of diagnosis, prognosis, and treatment. Automobile owners who can't pick up at least some rudiments of mechanics' argot run the risk of being cheated or ignored when they take their malfunctioning vehicles in for repair.

Conversely, specialists in technical accounts and codes commonly devote significant effort to either translating from conventions and stories into their own idioms or helping others make the translation. Paul Drew transcribes a fragment of conversation among a defense counsel (DC), a judge (J), and a defendant (D):

> DC: And after you knocked on the door, and prior to the time the door opened, was there any period of time elapsed?
> D: It seemed like three days to me.

J: I didn't hear.

D: Well, it seemed like three days of it and took so long to open the door. It seemed . . .

DC: And [clears throat] aside for the moment of how long it *seemed* to you, because of your then state of mind, do you have any, are you able to come to any estimate now with respect to real time? Was it a minute, was it a minute and a half? Or can you give us your best judgment. Not how long it seemed to you to have the door opened but how long it was. Just your best estimate.

D: Ah, hm, a minute and a half I suppose. (Adapted from Drew 2003: 918)

"It seemed like three days" could work perfectly well in casual conversation, but would never pass the test of a trial transcript. We catch the defense attorney in the act of translating from the language of convention into the idioms of codes. Watching medical interviews or religious catechisms, we can likewise witness translation from ordinary conversation into specialists' accounts. Still, the four types—conventions, stories, codes, technical accounts—distinguish forms of reason giving that most people encounter fairly often, and can easily tell apart.

Explaining Reasons

My job here is not to provide comprehensive, persuasive explanations of all the reasons that people give each other as they pursue their daily lives. In this small book it will be enough to try out preliminary answers to three questions:

1. Does social giving of reasons vary systematically (as I have just claimed) from popular to specialized and from formulas to cause-effect accounts? If it does, for example, we should discover that con-

ventions have family resemblances despite dramatic differences in cultural content, and that they differ visibly from technical accounts.

2. Do social relations between givers and receivers (again, as I have just claimed) strongly affect the reasons they propose, accept, or contest? If they do, for example, we should find that reason giving between professionals and their clients contrasts sharply with reason giving between spouses, and that professionals who provide technical services to their spouses therefore have trouble finding the right mode of communication.

3. Do negotiations over acceptable and unacceptable reasons differ significantly from one sort of social relation to another, as my arguments suggest they should? If they do, for example, we should notice that on average people argue harder about reasons when they disagree about the nature of their relationship, when the relation is intense, or when at least one of the parties has something to lose by acknowledging the character of the relation.

No one has yet analyzed sufficiently broad and ample evidence on reason giving to back definitive general answers to these questions. Still, an unexpected analogy helps make sense of variation in the giving and receiving of reasons. Reason giving resembles what happens when people deal with unequal social relations in general.[2] Participants in unequal social relations may detect, confirm, reinforce, or challenge them, but as they do so they deploy modes of communication that signal which of these things they are doing. In fact, the ability to give reasons without challenge usually accompanies a position of power. In extreme cases such as high public offices and organized professions, authoritative reason giving comes with the terri-

[2] Bashi Bobb 2001, Burguière and Grew 2001, Fitch 1998, Gould 2003, Schwartz 1975, Scott 1990, Tilly 2001.

tory.[3] Whatever else happens in the giving of reasons, givers and receivers are negotiating definitions of their equality or inequality.

Here are some possibilities that the analogy between negotiation of inequality and reason giving suggests:

- Within their own jurisdictions, professional givers promote and enforce the priority of codes and technical accounts over conventions and stories.
- In particular, professional givers generally become skilled at translating conventions and stories into their preferred idioms, and at coaching other people to collaborate in that translation.
- Hence the greater the professionalization of knowledge in any social setting, the greater the predominance of codes and technical accounts.
- To the extent that relations between giver and receiver are distant and/or giver occupies a superior rank, giver provides formulas rather than cause-effect accounts.
- Givers who offer formulas thereby claim superiority and/or distance.
- Receivers ordinarily challenge such claims, when they do, by demanding cause-effect accounts.
- Those demands typically take the forms of expressing skepticism about the proposed formula and asking for detail on how and why Y actually occurred.
- In the case of authoritatively delivered codes, however, a skilled receiver can also challenge the reasons given by deploying the code and demonstrating that giver has misused it.
- Even in the presence of distance and/or inequality, to the extent that receiver has visible power to affect giver's subsequent welfare, giver moves from formulas toward cause-effect accounts.

[3] Abbott 1988; Tilly 1998, chapter 5; Tilly and Tilly 1998, chapters 2 and 3.

In each case, acceptability of the reasons given depends on their match with the social relations that prevail between giver and receiver. Just as people involved in unequal relations regularly negotiate acceptable signals of deference or distinction, participants in reason giving maneuver in both directions: generally giving reasons that match the presumed relationship, but also signaling proposed definitions of the relationship by means of reasons given.

In principle, this interpretation could easily be wrong. If you think, for example, that most people give reasons based on their upbringing, group membership, fundamental beliefs, or deep-down character, you should expect people to offer the same reasons across a wide range of social circumstances. If you think, in contrast, that reason giving operates at two levels—deep, authentic reasons for intimate acquaintances differing from quick, convenient, opportunistic reasons for everyone else—you should not expect to see the sort of negotiation over relations that my account implies. In either case, then, available evidence could confirm that my claims fail to fit the facts. This book's arguments provide you with an opportunity to challenge them by drawing on your own experiences with the giving and receiving of reasons.

Here is what my account implies: Since most people engage in a wide variety of social relations, most people also implicitly carry around elaborate grids of conventions that fit one social situation or another; "Gotta go" can fittingly end a conversation with a chatty stranger who has stopped you to ask directions, but not a chance meeting with an old friend you haven't seen for years. Suppose that Alpha knocks Beta's book off a library table, then speaks one of the following lines:

Sorry, buddy. I'm just plain awkward.
I'm sorry. I didn't see your book.

Nuts! I did it again.

Why did you put that book there?

I told you to stack up your books neatly.

Each of these phrases implies a somewhat different relationship between Alpha and Beta.

Stories differ from conventions. They rely on (or at least claim) membership in a shared community of belief. Codes typically call up careful matching of the individuals involved with standardized identities—for example, prosecutor, defense attorney, judge, juror, defendant, and plaintiff—as well as relations among those identities. Technical accounts assume the auditor's belief in the reason-giver's competence. Hence the technical specialist's frequent display of authoritative markers: titles, certificates, white coats, professional tools, formidable desks.

In an extraordinary book about illness that will serve us well later on, Anatole Broyard describes waiting for the Boston urologist who would first diagnose his ultimately fatal prostate cancer:

> While I waited I subjected the doctor to a preliminary semiotic scrutiny.
> Sitting in his office, I read his signs. The diplomas I took for granted:
> What interested me was the fact that the room was furnished with taste.
> There were well-made, well-filled bookcases, an antique desk and chairs,
> a reasonable Oriental rug on the floor. A window opened one entire wall
> of the office to the panorama of Boston, and this suggested status, an
> earned respect. I imagined the doctor taking the long view out of his
> window. (Broyard 1992: 35)

To Broyard's great disappointment, the office did not belong to his urologist, who took him to another office that "turned out to be modern and anonymous. There were no antiques, no Oriental rug, and no pictures that I could see" (Broyard 1992: 35). By Broyard's high standards, the "impostor" failed to qualify as the physician of his hopes. But the story underlines the connections among standing, markers of that standing, and the capacity to issue credible technical accounts.

Not that lay observers automatically accept professional authority. Henry Petroski begins his superb analysis of engineering failures and successes with this anecdote:

> Shortly after the Kansas City Hyatt Regency Hotel skywalks collapsed in 1981, one of my neighbors asked me how such a thing could happen. He wondered, did engineers not even know enough to build so simple a structure as an elevated walkway? He also recited to me the Tacoma Narrows Bridge collapse, the American Airlines DC-10 crash in Chicago, and other famous failures, throwing in a few things he had heard about hypothetical nuclear power plant accidents that were sure to exceed Three Mile Island in radiation release, as if to present an open-and-shut case that engineers did not quite have the world of their making under control.
>
> I told my neighbor that predicting the strength and behavior of engineering structures is not always so simple and well-defined an undertaking as it might at first seem, but I do not think that I changed his mind about anything with my abstract generalizations and vague apologies. (Petroski 1992: 1)

The Hyatt Regency skywalk disaster of 1981 killed 114 people. That was the largest number of people ever to die in an American structure's collapse until 9/11 took its grim toll. In the press, the courts, professional journals, and general conversation the 1981 debacle generated stories, codes, and technical accounts alike, each feeding the others.

Failed expertise likewise promotes reason giving in medicine. As David Rothman documents, between the 1960s and the 1980s American medical doctors lost their hard-won ability to speak without challenge about the causes and cures of their patients' ills. They could less easily issue conventions or codes with the expectation that receivers would accept them passively. They lost some of their distance and superiority. Publicity concerning erroneous diagnoses and treatments, lawsuits on behalf of victims and survivors, political mobilization on behalf of patients, and the increasing intervention of legislators, insurers, bioethicists, and health maintenance organizations all inserted third parties into previously private—and quite one-sided—conversations between physicians and patients (Rothman 1991; see also Katz 2002).

Whether third parties intervene or not, technical reason-givers often find themselves shifting between their own technical accounts and acceptable explanations for exceptional events. Few recipients of technical bad news, for example, know enough engineering, medicine, or finance simply to absorb the language that practitioners of those specialties use to communicate precisely the same news among themselves. A standard textbook on interviewing for medical students sets it up this way:

> The first step in breaking bad news is assessing what the patient is ready to hear. The physician usually can do this by reviewing the clinical data, checking the patient's understanding and concerns about the data, and indicating that new information is available:
>
> PHYSICIAN: Mr. Virchow, you know that we saw a lump on the wall of your intestine and took a biopsy of it. What have you already learned about the results?
>
> Consider these possible responses:
>
> PATIENT: Well, is it cancer?
>
> PATIENT: Could you wait till my wife gets here? She gets off work at 6 o'clock.
>
> PATIENT: (silent, stares at the doctor's face)
>
> Patients who immediately ask if the diagnosis is cancer are ready to hear

the news. Others may indicate, verbally or nonverbally, that they are uncomfortable proceeding. For these patients, techniques to slow down the message may be appropriate. (Cole and Bird 2000: 212)

Cole and Bird's hypothetical physician would most likely be capable of giving a technical account of how colon cancers form. The physician in question could no doubt indicate, furthermore, which cause-effect relations within that account remain unclear or contested in the present state of knowledge. A physician's consultation on the case with colleagues generally follows just such protocols. He or she, however, rarely offers the patient a technical account. Although the textbook does not explicitly put it this way, the physician is transmitting a radically simplified technical account through two filters: one that translates the message into a language that the patient can interpret as reasons for an exceptional event, another that buffers the emotional shock of those reasons.

In their professional lives, physicians employ all the different varieties of reasons: conventions for routine problems, codes for their conformity to hospital rules, technical accounts for their consultations on difficult diagnoses, and stories for patients who lack the medical knowledge to follow the relevant technical accounts—not to mention stories physicians tell each other about cantankerous patients they have had to deal with. In some zone of expertise, however, almost every adult engages in the same sort of shifting among reasons. A New York taxi driver can give you a code for the extra fare he charges in the evening, a technical account of his circuitous path to your destination, a story for the music on his radio, or a conventional reason for his failure to follow your instructions. Most of us feel more comfortable challenging the reasons given by taxi drivers than those proposed by physicians. But in either case we are, among other things, negotiating definitions of the relations between us.

What's Coming

Pursuing this insight, the remainder of this book takes up different kinds of reasons in turn. Perhaps ironically, it proposes reasons for reasons. Chapters 2–5 take up conventions, stories, codes, and technical accounts in exactly that order. Chapter 6 closes the book by considering how technical specialists including social scientists can make their reason giving comprehensible to publics that lack familiarity with the technical problems of their disciplines.

Working as a historian and social scientist, I inevitably give more attention to historical and social scientific analysis than to other ways of thought. But I hope that by the end of the book even readers who have their doubts about the explanatory power of history and social science will gain insight into what happens when people in their own worlds start giving, receiving, and negotiating reasons. That's the reason for this book.

CONVENTIONS

Etiquette mixes propriety and self-interest. Listen to Peggy Post as she advises executives who want to make good use of their time: "If you have completed an appointment with someone who will not leave, rise and say, 'I'm terribly sorry, but I have some work that I must complete' " (Post 1997: 113). Successor of her great grandmother-in-law Emily Post and her mother-in-law Elizabeth Post as arbiter of etiquette for Americans who care about their manners and their business careers, Peggy Post must develop vicarious views of a great many situations she has surely never experienced herself. Among other things, she advises people in ticklish circumstances about giving reasons.

The problems Post helps resolve by means of good reasons include:

- discovering that you can't come to a dinner party you've already agreed to attend
- telling a child "no"
- distracting a job interviewer by blinking at the bright lights he has shining in your eyes
- informing your anxious parents why you are cohabiting, but not marrying
- explaining to your children why your companion has left
- refusing to shake hands because of your arthritis
- resigning a job that may be "too stressful or too boring, not adequately remunerative, or lacking in opportunity for advancement" (Post 1997: 142)

- extricating yourself from a long conversation by saying "Tom, I'm so glad to have had this chance to see you, but I've got to go or I'll be late for my next appointment (my carpool, nursery school pickup, the dentist, etc.). Say hello to Helen for me—good-bye!" (Post 1997: 286)

Here is a typical packet of Post advice:

You are never, in any way, except according to your own conscience, obligated to accept an invitation. Once having accepted, however, you must go. Nothing can change an acceptance to a regret except illness, death in the family or a sudden, unavoidable trip.

Furthermore, having refused one invitation on these grounds, you must not accept another more desirable one for the same day. You need give no excuse beyond "I'm afraid we are busy on the thirteenth," and *that* leaves you free to accept anything else that comes along. But if you have refused because you would be "out of town" and then you appear at a party attended by a mutual friend, you can certainly count on upsetting the senders of the first invitation. (Post 1997: 356–57)

A significant share of good etiquette, it turns out, consists of supplying appropriate, effective reasons why—for things you do, and for things you won't do. Good etiquette incorporates conventional reasons. The reasons need not be true, but they must fit the circumstances. On the whole, furthermore, in most circumstances that require polite behavior conventions work better than stories, codes, or technical accounts, which would only complicate the interchange. Conventions confirm or repair social relations.

From our point of view, stories, technical accounts, codes, and conventions all have secret lives. We concentrate here on how they serve the giving of reasons. But stories also amuse, threaten, and educate, whether or not their tellers are addressing serious "why" questions.

Technical accounts certainly incorporate explanations, but they also display their providers' expertise and signal where the experts stand on divisive questions within their fields. Codes likewise permit practitioners to make dazzling displays of knowledge and expertise, as well as to engage in breathtaking games of wit. Conventions, in their turn, mark boundaries between insiders and outsiders, fill lulls in conversations, and convey accumulated ideas from one generation to the next. In concentrating on reason giving, we are singling out just one way that people use conventions.

As we will soon see, nevertheless, conventions offered as reasons have far from trivial consequences. Defining social relations properly matters deeply for effective social life. Reasons, furthermore, justify practices—not merely attending or avoiding parties, but making or breaking friendships, granting or refusing favors, hiring or firing workers, even starting or ending wars. Supplying appropriate reasons for the situations and relationships at hand helps shape human social life as we know it. Supplying inappropriate reasons disrupts social life.

Peggy Post is therefore not simply telling tales about ideals. She is offering practical guidance for interacting with other people. From the 1950s through the 1970s, American social scientist Erving Goffman produced original, perceptive, influential studies of small-scale social interaction. (Goffman had not only a skeptical eye but a wry sense of humor; the first page of his *Relations in Public* [1971] bears the inscription, "Dedicated to the Memory of A. R. Radcliffe-Brown, whom on his visit to the University of Edinburgh in 1950 I almost met.") In his colorful studies, Goffman drew amply on his painfully acute personal observations and on carefully culled media accounts. But he also often cited books of etiquette, including those of Emily Post.

Goffman energetically defended his own use of Emily Post as an authority for his analyses of public behavior. He declared that etiquette books described norms actually influencing middle-class behavior and supplied "one of the few sources of suggestions about the structure of public conduct in America" (Goffman 1963: 5). As Goffman observed repeatedly, the ability to give appropriate reasons stands as a crucial sign of social competence. Conversely, the inability to give appropriate reasons ordinarily causes acute embarrassment. Goffman's analyses of what he called "accounts" concentrated on repair or concealment of publicly visible errors and derelictions, but the observation applies more generally to the conduct of social interaction.

Goffman pointed out, among other things, that improvised pantomimes sometimes serve as substitutes for the verbal giving of reasons; he called the practice "body gloss." Drawing on his students' observations, he offered these examples of body gloss:

A girl in a university dormitory, desiring to receive mail although no one is in correspondence with her, may see that she is observed going to the dormitory mailbox, gives the appearance of looking for a specific piece of mail that she presumably has been expecting, and on finding that it isn't there yet, shakes her head in puzzled wonderment—none of which she bothers doing when she thinks no one is observing her hopeless quest. A male participant at a get-acquainted dance, who would say (if he could get to talk to everyone) that he had merely dropped in this once, on his way someplace else, to see what it was like, feels it necessary to buy a drink to hold in his hand and to lean against one of the pillars, as if merely stopping by for a quick drink. A girl entering the table area of a ski lodge wanting to see and be seen by boys who might possibly pick her up, but not wanting to be precisely exposed in these aims, gives the appearance of looking for someone in particular, and she does this by grasping and fixing her sunglasses, which, in fact, remain well above her eyes resting on her hair. (Goffman 1971: 130)

Goffman characteristically concentrated on how individuals managed the impressions of themselves they gave to others rather than on the give-and-take of their interaction with other people. (The major exceptions to that rule occurred in his close studies of conversation, e.g., Goffman 1981.)

Even victims of mental illness, Goffman pointed out, devote major efforts to giving reaons. From his own interviews in a Washington, D.C., psychiatric hospital, he concluded that after the initial shock of incarceration, "With greater familiarity, each patient usually volunteers relatively acceptable reasons for his hospitalization, at the same time accepting without open immediate question the lines offered by other patients" (Goffman 1961: 152). From the interviews, for example, he extracted these explanations of different patients' commitment to the hospital:

> I was going to night school to get an M.A. degree, and holding down a job in addition, and the load got too much for me.
> The others here are sick mentally but I'm suffering from a bad nervous system and that is what is giving me these phobias.
> I got here by mistake because of a diabetes diagnosis, and I'll leave in a couple of days. [The patient had been in seven weeks.]
> I failed as a child, and later with my wife I reached out for dependency.
> My trouble is that I can't work. That's what I'm in for. I had two jobs with a good home and all the money I wanted. (Goffman 1961: 152–53)

Goffman heard people defining their relations with him and the hospital staff as those of normal people who had fallen into some sort of difficulty rather than as psychiatrically disturbed individuals.

Goffman's description reminds me of a long-past experience. About the same time that Goffman was observing in a Pennsylvania hospital, I was working as a research assistant at the ominously named Boston Psychopathic Hospital—"Boston Psycho" to us insiders. (In a day of euphemism, the name has now changed to Massachusetts Mental Health Center.) The big research institution took on challenging psychiatric cases, and shipped off people destined for long-term custody to other hospitals. My job consisted mainly of observing patient-patient and patient-staff interaction from a base in the occupational therapy division, with the idea that interpersonal relations themselves affected patients' well being. The job involved daily conversations with patients.

Patients at Boston Psycho often gave me reasons for their incarceration greatly resembling those on Goffman's list. Some patients, however, were so agitated or depressed that they did not carry on coherent conversations with passing researchers, and a few veterans accepted the medical definitions of their conditions. (In fact, Goffman points out that the Pennsylvania hospital staff and longer-term patients worked hard to challenge normalizing reasons and to push newcomers toward acceptance of their medical definitions; Goffman 1961: 154–55.) With these exceptions, reasons people gave me for their hospitalization generally constituted bids for acceptance of our person-to-person relation as that of normal people.

Goffman's extraordinary studies of self-presentation clearly underline one of this book's major points: although the giving of reasons—whether through words, pantomime, or the two together—enacts a kind of self-representation, it always does so in relation to others. A superficial reading of Goffman might give the impression that everything important happens inside individual psyches, that people are trying chiefly to reassure themselves and make sense of the world. Such a reading would greatly underestimate the significance of the people who receive an uneasy person's signals, and whose response to those signals the uneasy person is trying to manipulate or at least

anticipate. On the whole, Goffman's performing characters are trying to normalize their relations to other people.

Robert Edgerton's half-forgotten Goffmanesque study of coping
by mentally retarded persons who are concealing their condition
makes the point dramatically. These formerly hospitalized persons
have difficulty reading, counting money, and telling time, but cover
their incapacity by giving acceptable reasons. Edgerton calls those
reasons "serviceable excuses." "Fortunately," reports Edgerton,

> the ex-patients have developed serviceable excuses for most contingen-
> cies. For example, one woman was twice observed to excuse her inability
> to read labels in a market by saying that she had been drinking and
> couldn't focus her eyes very well. But one excuse is almost universally
> valid, and the ex-patients use it often. When the challenge to read can-
> not be avoided, the retardate simply fumbles about for an instant, then
> says that he's forgotten his glasses and can't see the words in question.
> The obliging normal usually can be depended on both to accept the
> excuse and to read aloud whatever is needed. (Edgerton 1967: 164)

Now and then I forget my reading glasses on a trip to the grocery
store. As a result, I can't decipher crucial labels. That makes a story
like Edgerton's quite plausible to me; if asked when wearing my
glasses, I would gladly help. Serviceable excuses normalize relations
among persons who might otherwise ignore or stigmatize each other.

A similar reason-giving strategy works for telling time:

> Instead of asking "What time is it?" the ex-patient asks, "Is it nine
> o'clock yet?" The answers to this question—"No, not for a few
> minutes," "It's way past nine," or "It's only eight"—are much less likely
> to be confusing. Consequently, the retardate usually asks for the time in
> this latter form, often holding up his or her own watch, saying "My
> watch stopped." Most of the retardates, even those who can't tell time,

wear watches. It helps greatly, in asking for the time, to be able to look at one's watch and ruefully remark that it has stopped running. As one man, who wears a long-inoperative watch, puts it: "I ask 'em, 'Is it nine yet?' and I say that my old watch stopped, and somebody always tells me how close it is to the time when I got to be someplace. If I don't have that old watch of mine on, people just act like I'm some kind of bum and walk away." (Edgerton 1967: 166)

Anyone who is reading this book can also read grocery labels and tell time. Yet all of us have had moments when we concealed our suddenly revealed incompetence by voicing—or miming—what we hoped was an appropriate reason: "Sorry, I thought this was Mr. Weber's office," "The sun got in my eyes," "This lock always sticks." As Goffman and Edgerton suggest, we often give reasons to avoid embarrassment. We prove that the relation between ourselves and others is not what it might seem to be.

Such reason giving does not, however, always support a claim of social competence. In some circumstances, the opposite occurs: the reasons offered explain a failure as a result of excusable incompetence. My watch stopped, so I can't tell what time it is. I forgot my glasses, and can't read this label. I'm sick, and therefore can't work today. I'm a stranger in town, and therefore can't help you find your way. I spent my last dollar on bus fare, and therefore have no money to give you. I have dyslexia, and therefore need extra time to take this test. Reason giving always defines, or redefines, the relationship between the parties. More precisely, it distinguishes the relationship between the parties from other relationships with which it would be risky, costly, confusing, or embarrassing to confuse it.

As Viviana Zelizer (2005) puts it, participants emphatically (if not always consciously) mark the boundaries among such adjacent relationships. Speaking particularly of relationships that combine monetary transactions with various forms of intimacy—courtship and prostitution come immediately to mind—Zelizer points out how participants strive to guard boundaries in both directions by means of distinctive practices and symbols. When the parties actually disagree—is this courtship, prostitution, or something in between?—trouble ensues. Reason giving then becomes part of negotiation over the proper definition of the relationship. Reasons mark the boundary.

How Conventions Work

Conventions differ from other reasons in two ways: their acceptance requires little or no technical knowledge, and they follow rules of appropriateness rather than of causal adequacy. They depend on widely recognizable formulas. Most of the time we can recognize the giving and receiving of conventional reasons by their stylized simplicity, and by the absence of further discussion. When a challenge arises, it usually does so not when the account is causally inadequate but when the receiver codes the reason given as inappropriate for the social relationship involved—for example, when psychiatrists reject a patient's normalizing account of his hospital admission. The receiver doesn't say "Don't tell me *that*," but "Don't tell *me* that!"

Etiquette, face-saving pantomime, psychiatric hospital admissions, and ruses of the mentally retarded confirm four major points about how conventions work:

1. The acceptability of such reasons does not depend on their truth, much less on their explanatory value, but on their appropriateness to the social situation.
2. In particular, conventions vary and take on acceptability—or unacceptability—largely according to the relationship between giver and receiver.

3. Nevertheless, the giving and acceptance of reasons has significant consequences for the parties and their relationship.

4. Among other consequences, reasons justify practices that would not be compatible with other reasons and/or definitions of the relationship.

Let us look more closely at the four principles.

Appropriateness of reasons to a social situation sorts out settings by what sorts of others are likely to observe the reason giving, and what sorts of inferences they are likely to make about the reasons' giver. Goffman's tales of body gloss show people projecting defensive images of themselves, images they would not bother to project if they thought themselves alone or invisible.

Goffman's body gloss also tells us that conventions do not necessarily employ words; symbols, objects, and body language will do. James Katz and Mark Aakhus give one example:

> Stopping at a Princeton, New Jersey, construction site, we half-consciously summarized the communicational situation. Before quite realizing it, we found in that buzzing, blooming confusion we could readily spot the person in charge. He was a man in his late 40s nestling a mobile phone in his meaty fist. The mobile phone was not what tipped us off—most workers at the site had cell telephones or pagers dangling from their belts. The boss carried his in his hand, its stubby antenna poking forward like an extra digit. . . . By otherwise occupying his hand with a mobile phone, he showed he had no intention of picking up a tool or performing manual labor. He used the phone's abbreviated antenna to point and gesture, in the manner of a nineteenth-century English army officer using his riding crop to dictate who needed to go where and do what. (Katz and Aakhus 2002: xx)

Reading Katz and Aakhus, I suddenly realized that I had unconsciously adopted a similar effective reason-giving strategy. Many of you, my readers, have probably adopted the same strategy. Often someone knocks on my windowless office door when I am talking on the telephone. For years, when that happened I explained to my caller what was happening, set down the phone, walked to the door, opened it, and asked the visitor to wait until I finished my call, then went back to the phone; total time for the transaction: about a minute. During calls, I also often found myself setting down the phone to fetch a book, a paper, or a file from beyond my reach, and sometimes broke the connection in the process.

In a fit of inspiration, one day I went to a nearby Radio Shack and bought a coiled twenty-five foot telephone cord, replaced the old short cord, and that little aspect of my life changed. Not only could I now continue a conversation as I searched for relevant material, but also when I went to answer the door I still had the telephone at my ear, my visitor saw instantly that I had a caller, usually signaled an apology for interrupting us, and always indicated that she or he would wait outside. I no longer had to speak my reasons. Of course, if the visitor was a close friend I hadn't seen for some time, I still interrupted the call to apologize, explain what was happening, and (depending on the nature of the call) either asked the person in to await the call's end or indicated where my friend could wait. With most visitors, nevertheless, a clutched telephone substituted for words.

I would have to adopt a different reason-giving strategy if I were using a cell phone on the street and met a friend. Friends I meet on the street when they are talking on their own cell phones often smile, wave, and keep on talking. If they are likely to see me again later, the smile and wave suffice to say that they are too busy right now to talk with me. Settings matter for the giving of conventional reasons. Relevant settings vary in at least these regards:

> from decorous (e.g., a church) to informal (e.g., a park)
> from public (e.g., the street) to private (e.g., your own kitchen)

from impersonal (e.g., an office) to intimate (e.g., your family home)
from foreign (e.g., a new city) to familiar (e.g., the old neighborhood)

Imagine yourself suffering a sudden attack of nausea in each pair of settings, and wanting to tell others present why you are rushing for the nearest receptacle. In each case, the cause is the same, but appropriate reasons are different.

Political climate also affects the appropriateness of reasons people give in public. Philip Moss and my son, labor economist Chris Tilly, conducted or supervised hundreds of interviews with employers of relatively unskilled workers in Detroit, Los Angeles, Atlanta, and Boston. They were trying to find out to what extent and how screening practices incorporated judgments about racial and ethnic differences in skills, broadly defined as individual characteristics that would affect job performance. They soon learned that prospective employers consider not only learned cognitive and technical abilities but also "soft skills," including interaction style and motivation, as relevant criteria for hiring. Employment officers often believe that soft skills differ significantly from one ethnic-racial category to another.

During the politically correct 1990s, however, no employer would cite personal preference for one ethnic-racial category or another as a reason for hiring. As Moss and Tilly put it:

Not one employer told us, "I don't like blacks" or "I prefer to hire someone from my own ethnic group." But many, many managers made statements like "Blacks are less reliable" or "Immigrants work harder." Nobody said, "I didn't want to start up my business in a Latino neighborhood," but plenty claimed, "If we located in the inner city, we'd still have to attract a workforce from the suburbs." Statements like these combine objective assessments of workforce skills with racial stereotypes, and it is very hard to draw the line between the two. (Moss and Tilly 2001: 4)

Since the persistent interviewers were educated strangers who asked explicit questions about race and ethnicity in hiring, employers found themselves in a public situation. In telephone interviews, when asked in general about categorical differences, employers rarely identified any. Yet in face-to-face interviews, similar employers often gave acceptable categorical reasons: significant average differences in hard or soft skills. Asked to explain such differences, they typically turned not to genes or culture but to education, family structure, alternative job opportunities, contact with welfare, neighborhood influences, and previous work experience—in short, the same sorts of reasons that prevail in public discussions of racial and ethnic inequality.

Still, the employers that Moss and Tilly interviewed certainly didn't talk like social scientists:

> Spanish people are more willing to work. They are willing to work longer hours. I think the ones that I've known are very dedicated to their jobs. [*Boston-area metal-finishing shop*]
> Your Asian workforce, because it's the newest immigrant in the country, and what I've seen with them is they have a completely different work ethic. You need them for seventy-two hours a day, they'll be there for seventy-two hours a day. [*Boston-area factory*] (Moss and Tilly 2001: 117)

Moss and Tilly realized, of course, that they were asking delicate questions. Here is a segment of an interview with a clerical supervisor in an Atlanta-area educational institution:

> INTERVIEWER: A number of the people that we have talked to in the area have commented on the differences between black and white workers. Could you comment on that?
> RESPONDENT: [whispers inaudible words]
> INTERVIEWER: But it's confidential.
> RESPONDENT: I know, I know. I guess you hear me hedging a little. It

just depends on the individuals. But this has been one of our problems. The . . . a lot of it is the . . . and it's not true, blanket . . . definitely it's not, but unfortunately in the majority of the cases we have problems that tend to be minority. I am going to close my door in case anyone comes down the hall. (Moss and Tilly 2001: 120)

Respondents, obviously, worried about giving the wrong reasons. But the researchers also faced a serious problem as they tried to distinguish stated reasons from "true" reasons. Like many social researchers, they were trying to derive (or at least to check) technical accounts by means of evidence supplied in the form of conventions. But for our purposes they made a discovery of capital importance: appropriate reasons varied significantly with the social situation.

The findings of Moss and Tilly go farther, however. Within any class of social situations, the *match to the relationship* carries weight that goes beyond general decorum. Significant others are not only forming general impressions of the reason-giver; they are also evaluating the message sent about the character of their relationship. Acceptable conventions differ wildly depending on whether the relationship is doctor-patient, wife-husband, previously unacquainted fellow passengers on a train, members of a sports team, police officer-citizen, or student-teacher. "Sorry, officer, I didn't see the sign" may satisfy the traffic cop, but not, ironically, your spouse. In the Moss and Tilly interviews, employment officers matched their reasons carefully with their relationship to academically based researchers.

Appropriate reasons vary dramatically with the equality, inequality, and intimacy or distance of the relationship. A superior speaking to an inferior need give no more than perfunctory reasons for actions that damage or threaten the inferior; even parents speaking to their rebellious children sometimes resort to "Because I say so!" An inferior speaking to a superior must often offer defensible reasons coupled with apologies—however truthful and heartfelt—for failures and misdeeds; "Sorry, Boss, I just wasn't thinking" illustrates this mode. Equals generally owe each other reasons having at least the appearance of mutual consideration, in the vein of "Excuse me, I didn't see you waiting for me."

In his searching examination of doctor-patient relations, physician Jay Katz describes a conversation in which he and a surgeon reviewed the many uncertainties in current knowledge of therapies for breast cancer. Katz then asked the surgeon how he would speak to a patient who faced a choice of treatments. The colleague told of an actual interview with a patient a few days earlier: "At the beginning of their encounter, he had briefly mentioned a number of available treatment alternatives. He added that he had done so without indicating that any of the alternatives to radical surgery deserved serious consideration. Instead, he had quickly impressed on his patient the need for submitting to this operation" (Katz 2002: 166–67). Katz reminded him of the uncertainties they had just discussed, but the surgeon insisted that radical surgery was the best treatment. Asked about his own approach, Katz replied that he would discuss the alternatives at length with the patient, discover her preferences, and arrive at a joint decision through informed negotiation. The surgeon countered with the claims that patients lack the necessary knowledge, that patients were likely to choose treatments for the wrong reasons, and that such choices would cause the patient unnecessary pain—in short, that he knew better. In their conversation, Katz and his surgeon friend were contrasting relatively unequal and relatively equal views of the doctor-patient relationship, and disputing the physician's proper giving of reasons on precisely that ground.

But, whether equal or unequal, the location of a relationship in the range from distant to intimate also matters deeply to reason giving. Distant relationships justify perfunctory reasons, and render elaborate reasons incomprehensible, intrusive, or embarrassing. The more intimate the relationship, in contrast, the more detailed the reasons one party usually expects from the other, and the more vulnerable the reason giver to the demand that he back up challenged conventions with a story, a code, or even a technical account. Lovers owe each other more elaborate reasons, and reasons more consistent with their other interactions, than fellow jurors do.

The pressure to give reasons that match relationships is so strong and universal that we rarely notice ourselves performing the match. The matching of reason with relationship becomes much more visible, however, in the case of mismatches. Studying how people negotiate interpersonal trust, sociologists Linda Weber and Allison Carter interviewed nineteen women and twenty men from their teens to their fifties about recent close relationships. They report the story of a young woman, Shelley, and her boyfriend:

> Like things were just like, everything was, we just got really close because we had so much in common it was just like, it was like, oh God, it's really weird to find somebody like that. And he just totally stopped calling and it was like, I deserve an explanation. And I finally got one like three weeks later, but I had to hunt him down for the explanation. And he gave me the explanation and that's just fine and dandy but you know, I'm gone. He had somebody else coming back into his life and [she] put an ultimatum on him. . . . So we had a really long discussion. He understood what I was thinking and he was like, well, you know what the funny part is? I'm like, what? He goes, I was going to choose you. I said, wrong. You didn't have a choice. I'm like, the first day that passed that you didn't return my call that was when your choice ended. And he was like, but you kept calling. Your choice ended, I said, I wanted an explanation and I deserved one. (Weber and Carter 2003: 53)

Shelley did not reject the inconstant boyfriend's reason giving because it was false. She rejected his reasons because they defined their relationship as one in which he had the option of offering or with-drawing his attention, while she did not.

That brings us back to our third principle: as in relations between Shelley and her former boyfriend, reason giving has *consequences* for subsequent interactions. The consequences range from trivial (a moment of irritation) to serious (a lifetime of condemnation or separation). Reason giving has consequences both because it proposes a definition for the relationship and because it justifies the practices of one party toward the other. Reasons, relationships, and practices align.

How Emergency Room Workers Use Reasons

In many organizations, reason giving plays a significant part in the allocation of advantages and disadvantages. Toward 1970, Julius Roth and his research team observed six hospital emergency rooms in the Northeast and on the West Coast. They were trying to see how emergency service workers' judgments of patients' moral fitness affected the treatment those patients received. They discovered plenty of categorizing—for example, differential treatment of supposed alcoholics and street people. They found that already being a patient of a doctor attached to the hospital significantly improved the patient's chances of rapid, effective attention.

Roth and his collaborators also found medical personnel distinguishing sharply between services that belonged and did not belong to their jobs—between legitimate and illegitimate requests for help. "The negative evaluation of patients is strongest," reports Roth "when they combine an undeserving character with illegitimate demands. Thus, a patient presenting a minor medical complaint at an inconvenient hour is more vigorously condemned if he is a welfare case than if he is a 'respectable citizen' " (Roth 1972: 849). Even in the moment of crisis, medical staff and patients were implicitly negotiating appropriate definitions of their relationships.

Reason giving figured importantly in those definitions. It justified differential treatment:

Nursing staff in proprietary hospitals dealing with the private patients of attending physicians do not have as authoritative a position vis-à-vis their clients as public hospital staff have; therefore, the demands for prompt compliance with staff directions must be used sparingly. In such a case more surreptitious forms of control are used. The most common device is keeping the patient waiting at some step or steps in his processing or treatment. Since the patient usually has no way of checking the validity of the reason given for the wait, this is a relatively safe way that a nurse can control the demands made on her and also serves as a way of "getting even" with those who make inappropriate demands or whom she regards as undeserving for some other reason. (Roth 1972: 854–55; see also Schwartz 1975, chapter 5)

Roth's observations resonate with my own observations (more extensive than I would like) in hospital emergency rooms. Conscious patients propose reasons for their being there, family members propose reasons for unconscious patients, triage nurses sort out reasons and supply reasons of their own, the chaos of the treatment area resounds with reason giving, as the reasons given and accepted vary dramatically with the relationship between giver and receiver.

New York-based *Times Literary Supplement* correspondent Michael Greenberg relates a trip to the emergency room with his perpetually suffering older brother, Steve:

That evening he phones me in a state of panic. He tumbled to the floor on his way to the bathroom and had to cry out until a neighbour came to help him get up. I rush back to his apartment and drag him to the hospital emergency room. An administrator taps his name into the computer, and frowns. Evidently, in recent years Steve has shown up several times with "imaginary ailments." In each instance he was perfunctorily discharged. Now we are put at the bottom of the list, last in the hierarchy of illness. After five or six hours, we are led to an inner sanctum where a CAT scan is taken of Steve's brain. It proves to be normal, and we are sent on our way. (Greenberg 2004: 16)

A computer spit out information that contradicted reasons provided by the patient and his younger brother; as a result, they waited and waited.

Emergency room reason giving alternates among all four kinds of relational work that I distinguished in chapter 1: creation of new relations, confirmation of existing relations, negotiating shared definitions of the relations at hand, and repairing damaged relations. Most often, suffering patients and their escorts accept the expert-patient definition proposed to them by the local staff; they behave properly as compliant patients, accepting the reasons staff members offer them. The convention by which patients have first names only, but physicians become Dr. ___ reinforces the inequality.

Sometimes, however, patients or their advocates negotiate definitions of the relationship, as when a patient placed in the "not serious" category pleads for recognition as seriously ill. Occasionally, one party offers reasons to repair a damaged relationship—for example, in cases where the hospital staff apologizes for initially treating an influential person or someone suffering a neural disorder as a common drunk. As a patient in university hospital emergency rooms, I have sometimes witnessed a dramatic improvement in my treatment—and the prevailing definition of our relationship—when the staff discovered my identity as a professor in the university that ran the hospital.

Emergency room observations also confirm our fourth principle: *reasons justify practices that would not be compatible with other reasons and/or definitions of the relationship.* Up to this point, I have simplified my account of reason giving by speaking as though parties agree on the nature of their relationship, and accordingly find the appropriate reasons to match the relationship. Most of the time it works that way; early in life, socially effective people learn to give the right reasons for the setting and relationship. Yet the cases of employment officers, estranged couples, and emergency rooms add an important twist. Often invisibly, but sometimes visibly and angrily, parties to a relationship are negotiating both its definition and the practices that belong to it as they interact. At the extreme, in defense of a valued practice or privilege, one of the parties denies a relationship that would otherwise apply: "sorry, friend, but business is business," "rules are rules," "I'm bound by higher loyalties," and so on. In these cases, one party is justifying practices that disappoint or damage the other party.

Such practices and their matched reasons matter. As a longtime college teacher, I have sometimes had to judge students' reasons for late, missing, misunderstood, botched, or apparently plagiarized assignments. No one has ever told me, "The dog ate my homework," but many a term paper has apparently disappeared in a flood, a theft, or a hard disk failure. My judgment (and often our negotiation) concerning the reasons proposed placed at risk their grades, their class standings, their graduations, or in extreme cases their continuation in school. Still, on the whole my acceptance or rejection of students' reasons has not seriously affected their welfare.

My service as paymaster for a U.S. Navy amphibious squadron during the Korean War, in contrast, went differently: handling other people's money made the whole business more serious. When payday came around, it is true, I had no choice but to hand out cash the men—there were no women—on my eight small ships had coming. I loaded money from my safe into a big leather box, my petty officers and I strapped on loaded .45 caliber pistols, then we went from ship

to ship, setting up payday. I paid whether I had good relations with
the recipients or not. As each man signed his receipt, I counted out
exactly in cash the amount my clerks' calculations showed he was
due. In that rule-bound situation, reasons mattered little—or, better,
we all took reasons for granted.

On other occasions, however, I enjoyed surprising discretion. Sail-
ors often came in with requests for advances in pay to deal with personal emergencies or for money to cover official travel, complete with
reasons. But the government issued changes in relevant regulations
almost daily. We, the local custodians of the regulations, had either
to pen in, initial, and date corrections to our local copy of the rules
or substitute new pages that came to us from the central authorities.
Our operating manual looked like a well-marked, unabridged dic-
tionary in a giant looseleaf binder.

I soon discovered that the rules' complexity and changeability gave
me a powerful advantage: because my petty officers and I were the
only ones who actually knew the rules and because I was personally
liable for faulty payments, if a request arrived from an importunate
sailor at a bad time, I could usually find a legal reason to refuse payment. I could behave like the Ragionier Ciampan, who swore on the
hefty rulebook that city law forbade him to authorize my photo-
graphing documents in the Milan archives. Of course, if the commo-
dore, my squadron's commanding officer, needed a travel advance,
he usually got it. Power limited my ability to adjudicate reasons, and
to reject other people's reasons as inappropriate.

Justifying Practices

How does the alignment among reasons, relationships, and practices
work? They actually form a triangle of the following sort:

Most of the time, people match reasons to relationships without much trouble. The trouble begins with either of two circumstances: first, the reason given implies a relationship one of the parties contests, or, second, one of the parties is using the reason to justify a contested practice. Earlier we saw Shelley contesting the reasons proposed by her ex-boyfriend because the reasons defined their relationship in an unacceptable way; her objections illustrate the first circumstance. But as a paymaster, my discovery of legal objections to a payment exempted me from doing a friendly favor. I put myself in the second circumstance: justifying a contested practice.

Justification sometimes occurs in all types of reason giving: not only conventions, but also stories, technical accounts, and codes. Justification by means of conventions, however, has a peculiar property: participants rarely take the reason proposed seriously as a cause-effect account, and more often treat it as a characterization of the relationship, the practices, and the connection between them. A good reason offers an acceptable characterization.

In an influential study of abortion and contraception, Kristin Luker saw three versions of the triangle intersecting: how women and men who were seeking an abortion reported the interplay of reasons and practices in their own relationship; how Luker's relationship to the people she interviewed affected that reporting; and how Luker herself finally understood the connections among relationships, reasons, and practices.

In 1969, Luker worked as an intake interviewer in a suburban California contraceptive clinic. During a two-month period, among many other applicants for contraception or therapeutic abortion, she interviewed three people whose contraceptive behavior surprised her:

white, middle-class, non-Catholic women who had already received an abortion during the previous six months. The three women came to the clinic because they thought they might be pregnant, and might therefore need another abortion. Since the women had received contraceptive instruction after the previous abortion, were not trying to land a husband, and were not obviously psychiatrically disturbed, the most widely accepted reasons then accepted for resort to abortion—ignorance, class, race, religion, mental aberration, and/or failed courtship—did not apply.

The anomalies spurred Luker to start her own study of clients who came to a northern California contraception-abortion clinic sponsored by Planned Parenthood/World Population. She did her work in two stages: analyzing the medical records of the first five hundred women who attended the clinic, then interviewing fifty of the women, sometimes in the company of husbands or lovers, plus ten women under the care of a private practitioner in the Bay Area. (In a few cases, she also interviewed husbands or lovers separately.) Luker only interviewed women who had previously used contraception, and who despite their contraceptive knowledge had consciously taken the risk of conception; by their own lights, these women were "taking chances." One interchange went like this:

> INTERVIEWER: What kind of contraception were you using?
> RESPONDENT: We were using rhythm, which was also ridiculous considering we knew what could happen—what *did* happen. It's amazing that two supposedly bright people could get into this twice. (Luker 1975: 132)

It became less "amazing" in a number of cases, however, because the contraceptive technology available around 1970 centered on condoms, withdrawal, rhythm, an antiovulation pill taken in advance, intrauterine devices installed by a physician, and foams or douches administered immediately after intercourse. For cohabiting couples, all the choices depended to some extent on consent and cooperation—they depended on the relationship:

> INTERVIEWER: How did he feel about using rhythm?
> RESPONDENT: We were being puritanical because we didn't want to use artificial things.
> INTERVIEWER: Artificial?
> RESPONDENT: Just a chemical effect on your body or having something inserted in you. (Luker 1975: 43)

Reasons, practices, and relationships clearly interacted. Sexual partners were defining their relations to each other.

Not only relationships between the sexual partners mattered, however. Third parties sometimes loomed large—for example, in the case of individuals or couples from Catholic families. Even in the absence of Catholic prohibitions, interpersonal networks made a difference:

> INTERVIEWER: You said that you had used the pill previously and had run out. Where did you get the pills the first time?
> RESPONDENT: A family planning clinic in Southwest City.
> INTERVIEWER: Why didn't you get the prescription refilled?
> RESPONDENT: Because of my father . . . We live in a small town, and the medical and dental people are very close, and I couldn't go to another doctor without his finding out and I think it would hurt him. (Luker 1975: 44)

Luker gained insight into the relationship-reason-practice triangle twice. First, the women described how their relations with their male partners worked and produced their (noncontraceptive) practices. Second, with an edge of justification they also discussed their practices in relation to Luker, a sympathetic but obviously knowledgeable young woman.

Reflection on the first two cycles led Luker to her own analysis of connections among relations, reasons, and practices. She concluded sensibly that many different paths led contraception-savvy women to unwanted pregnancies. But most of those paths had three things in common:

- Social (and not only sexual) interactions with their partners raised the perceived costs of contraception.
- Couples' estimates of the risks of conception declined gradually as they continued to use risky practices without pregnancy.
- The women, and sometimes the couples, came to think of abortion as a viable alternative in case they became pregnant.

The couples adjusted their reasons and practices as their relationships evolved. At any given point in the evolution, however, the reasons cohabiting couples gave themselves or others for their contraceptive (or noncontraceptive) practices constituted justifications more than they involved cause-effect explanations. The relationship-reason-practice triangle continued to operate.

Reasons in War Plans

The triangle operates at a larger scale, and with even more portentous consequences, than these tales of love affairs, emergency rooms, military service, and abortion clinics reveal. It affects American war plans. In a complex but illuminating book, Stanford sociologist and military analyst Lynn Eden has studied the place of thinking about fire damage in American nuclear planning since World War II. From the bombing of Hiroshima and Nagasaki onward, informed observers had seen evidence that in urban areas bomb-induced fire produced even more death and destruction than did the initial blast itself. Yet to the present day, military planners have regularly ex-

cluded fire damage from their calculations of damage inflicted by
nuclear weapons, hence from their nuclear strategies. They calculated likely damage exclusively in terms of what the initial blast would
do. Among many other effects, the exclusion at least doubled prevailing estimates of the firepower required for a given amount of destruction. That probably means the armed forces requested weapons levels
at least twice as high—and twice as expensive—as would actually have
fulfilled a given nuclear plan. Your taxes and mine paid the price.

How could that happen? Like Luker, Eden builds her own cause-
effect technical account, a variety of reason giving we will look at
more closely later. Seeking reasons for the neglect of fire, Eden rules
out the obvious suspects:

- that (as many experts long maintained) fire damage was too unpre-
  dictable for incorporation into military doctrine
- that (as many of the same experts long maintained) blast damage was
  so extensive as to make fire damage secondary
- that available evidence of fire damage was too weak for confident
  extrapolation
- that existing computers couldn't handle the problem's complexity
- that incendiary warfare was so immoral or psychologically repellent
  as to deter thinking about it
- that the Air Force had an organizational interest in understating nuclear damage, and thereby promoting larger investments in weapons
  and air power

Instead, Eden argues that military organizational structures and
processes themselves produced military blindness with regard to fire
effects. She draws on parallels from studies of nonmilitary organizational behavior and of scientific laboratories to build a fresh account
of military self-deception. She also uses the idea of frames, brought
into the social sciences by Erving Goffman (Goffman 1974). She

shows how the very structures of organizations establish frames that focus attention on some kinds of information while screening out a great deal of other information that could, in principle, significantly affect their operation. Although she doesn't put it this way, she also shows how reasons that make sense in a given set of relationships (even though they would look strange in other settings) justify practices in military organizations, as they do elsewhere.

Some engineers and physicists (including a number that Eden interviewed) knew a good deal about fire damage from World War II surveys of incendiary bombing forward. They found American nuclear doctrine on the subject surprising, even alarming. But those experts did not catch the military eye. The organizations that had so successfully used air power during World War II moved into peacetime, and then into the Cold War, with organization-built blinders in place:

The assumptions most deeply ingrained in the air force during the war—that specific industrial and other installations as parts of critical target systems were to be destroyed by the blast effects of air-dropped *conventional* weapons—carried over to the understanding of *atomic* weapons in the immediate postwar period: Specific installations were to be targeted, and the relevant mechanism would be blast. The association of precision bombing and blast damage was a historical one. Because of the early priority of precision bombing in World War II, greater knowledge had been developed about blast damage than fire damage, making blast damage more predictable by the end of the war. These understandings of what would be targeted and what would be the means of destruction served as the basis for the organizational capabilities developed, the knowledge acquired, and the routines invented regarding prediction of damage in the postwar period. (Eden 2004: 93–94)

In a parallel development, the American community of fire prevention experts assimilated the analysis of nuclear-bomb fire to their
previously existing knowledge and practices regarding ground-initi-
ated fires. They did not recognize, for example, that a nuclear blast
creates its own powerful winds, which propel fire beyond the blast
site. As a consequence, knowledgeable fire engineer Horatio Bond
could not awaken his professional colleagues to the distinctiveness
of fire effects in nuclear attacks, despite making the effort from the
late 1950s (Eden 2004: 199). He could not get his bundle of reasons
and practices across.

If this all seems remarkably shortsighted, take a good look at the
organizations in which you spend your time. I have worked about
half of my professional career teaching in large public universities. If
you look carefully at a large public university, you will soon discover
how many institutional arrangements build in assumptions about the
likely futures, educational capacities, and personal preferences of
vanished generations—and how hard it is to get information about
the actual effects of those arrangements. Try looking at the educa
tional rationales for intercollegiate football, undergraduate majors,
and scholastic aptitude tests!

The interplay among reasons, relationships, and practices matters
in the nuclear damage case because American military organization
decisively channeled who talked to whom, who was a credible interlocutor, and therefore how reasons and practices coincided. As late
as 1992, Vice Admiral Michael Colley, vice director of the Joint Strategic Target Planning Staff, terminated scientifically backed attempts
to incorporate fire effects into standard models of nuclear damage.
Asked about that decision in 1993, he told Eden that in Russia, still
the prime target of nuclear attack doctrine, fire effects remained un-
predictable. When Eden sought his reaction to high-level briefings
on recent scientific work presented late in 1991, Colley replied: "The

briefing, in all honesty, Lynn, was not important to me. . . . It was my evaluation that we could spend our money better elsewhere. . . . To me, it was just one more of this continuing pileup of things that we ought not to be spending money on, because we didn't need to. It didn't *add* anything to our effectiveness. The attack was *devastating* and complete as it was" (Eden 2004: 271–72). In short, implied the admiral, if the point is to destroy selected sites by means of precision bombing, what matters is to choose means you're sure will destroy them. Side effects such as fire don't matter for that decision. Relevant reasons for targeting nuclear weapons in one way or another concern the impact of blast on critical enemy targets. At the end of 2004, semiofficial U.S. estimates concerning the likely impact of an Indian-Pakistani nuclear war still reflected exactly that principle: only blast matters (Batcher 2004).

Again, any of us who works with "this continuing pileup of things" in a less powerful organization than the U.S. Defense Department can sympathize with the beleaguered admiral. So many demands are competing for our attention! But that is the point: which demands, which reasons, which relationships, and therefore which sorts of reliable information reach us depend on historically established organizational routines over which we exercise limited control. When conventions work, they do so because they fit appropriately into local conditions, not because they offer adequate explanations of what actually happens locally. Most of the time, we bolster accepted practices with conventions. That's how we keep valuable relations with others operating smoothly.

Conventions, however, don't always keep things running smoothly. Sometimes people call for codes or technical accounts from experts who specialize in such matters. Much more often, people confronted with puzzling, unexpected, dramatic, problematic, or exemplary events turn to stories. Let's see where stories take us.

STORIES

During the 1970s, Jerry Falwell came to national attention as a leading American television preacher and fundamentalist institution-
builder. In 1979, he established the Moral Majority as a significant
force in American conservative politics. By 1984, he headed the
Thomas Road Baptist Church and the very religious Liberty University in Lynchburg, Virginia, while running radio and television's *Old-
Time Gospel Hour* and its associated publishing house. Falwell and his
faithful followers insisted on the Christian Bible's literal truth and
espoused strict creationism as they adamantly opposed both abortion
and homosexuality. Falwell's vivid preaching identified him and his
followers closely with biblical characters who struggled against hardship, faced temptation, faltered repeatedly, but conquered with God's
grace. Bible readers could easily recognize the formula. The message
backed Falwell's incessant appeals for financial support: sacrifice for
a sacred cause. But it also shaped Falwell's presentation of his personal life story.

Take his account of racial integration in his congregation. Falwell
denied he was ever a racist, but until 1968 he supported racial segregation in his religious institutions. He also denied that Congress, the
courts, or civil rights activists changed his mind during the 1960s. He
publicly opposed Lyndon Johnson's civil rights legislation of 1964. At
that point, he reported,

> I felt bullied and unjustly attacked by the army of white Northerners
> marching into the South, demanding that we follow their dictates in the
> running of our community and in the ordering of our lives. I was angry

that suddenly the Supreme Court, the Congress, and the President had
assumed rights once granted to the states, and I protested loudly the
arrogant, disruptive, and often violent wave of demonstrators arriving
daily in the South. I was determined to maintain the right to decide for
ourselves how we would live together, black and white. (Falwell 1997:
312–13)

But, he claimed, God was already undermining his commitment to
racial segregation. Falwell told this story:

Then one Saturday morning in 1963 I sat in the end chair of Lee Bacas's
shoeshine business on Main Street in Lynchburg. It was my Saturday
morning ritual to have Lewis, an elderly black man, shine my shoes at
10 AM. He could set his watch by my appearance in his chair.

"I heard your sermon on television last week, Reverend," Lewis said
as he began dusting a week of dirt off my shoes. "I sure do like the way
you preach."

"Why thank you, Lewis," I replied, looking closely at the thin, muscu-
lar man in his middle sixties whose curly gray hair framed his shiny,
smiling face. "How are you and the Lord getting on?" I asked him,
knowing already the answer.

"So good," he replied, grinning up at me. "The Lord is so good,
isn't he?"

Every week Lewis shared his faith with me. And every week I left his
chair feeling his ministry in my life. Then on that particular Saturday
morning Lewis asked a question that he had never asked before.

"Say, Reverend," he began softly, so that no one else could hear,
"when am I going to be able to join that church of yours over on
Thomas Road?"

Once again I felt like a boxer who had been punched directly in the
stomach. For the first time in years, I was speechless. We had a growing
number of black families who had heard me preach on television or radio

who stopped by to visit Thomas Road on occasion, but never once had one of them asked the question that Lewis had just asked me.

"I don't want to cause you no trouble, Reverend," the old man said as he finished polishing my shoes and helped me down from the chair, "but I sure do like the way you preach and would like one day to join there with you."

I puzzled over the question that next week and in the months that followed. I had no good reason that Lewis could not join my church. He was kind enough not to ask me for an explanation, because he knew there was none. I had excuses, but I had no reasons. (Falwell 1997: 317–18)

Falwell described that moment as "God's still small voice in my heart" (Falwell 1997: 315). Yet the voice he heard in 1963 took long years to register: Falwell founded the segregated Lynchburg Christian Academy in 1967, and Thomas Road Baptist Church did not admit its first black members until 1968. Despite pressure from other religious leaders, furthermore, the Academy accepted no black students until 1969. Lewis himself stayed with his black Baptist church until his death (Falwell 1997: 320–21). Nevertheless, said Falwell, "God may have used the Congress and the courts, the strident marchers and their noisy demonstrations to get my attention, but He used the quiet loving voice of Lewis to open up my heart and to help bring lasting change to me and to my ministry" (Falwell 1997: 321).

In his sermons, Falwell often relied on reasons best described as conventional, frequently turned to codes from theology, and occasionally presented the technical accounts of creation science, his church's alternative to evolutionary theory. But repeatedly he laid out lessons with something like his shoeshine tale's structure: someone else's action or remark makes the Christian hero aware of his failings, the stricken hero seeks divine inspiration, and the hero changes course (Harding 2000). He told stories.

Not just televangelists tell stories. Interviewers, for example, often elicit stories. Religiously active middle-class homemaker Betty Dyson, married eleven years with two children, offered interviewer Ann Swidler this account of her courtship:

> As for why I married the person I did, he was the right person at the right time at the right place. We met while we were going to school and we spent a lot of time together and we decided fairly quickly that we wanted to be married and share our lives . . .
> He's an awful lot like my father. I'm an awful lot like his mother. He was the kind of person I felt I could share a lot with, who had similar ideas and a similar outlook. We were very compatible. We enjoyed doing a lot of the same things. We were good friends. (Swidler 2001: 114–15)

As Swidler says, her interviewees drew on widely available cultural repertoires as they provided such accounts, but they created their own stories without enormous concern for accuracy or consistency. Stories of how people loved and married always involve explanations of a sort, with at least a tinge of justification. And they vary with the audience.

Virtues of Stories

Stories provide simplified cause-effect accounts of puzzling, unexpected, dramatic, problematic, or exemplary events. Relying on widely available knowledge rather than technical expertise, they help make the world intelligible. As in Falwell's account of reasons for his institutions' desegregation, they often carry an edge of justification or condemnation. They qualify as a special sort of narrative, which a standard manual on the subject defines as "the representation of an event or a series of events" (Abbott 2002: 12). This particular variety of narrative includes actors, their actions, and effects produced by those actions. The story usually gives pride of place to human actors. When the leading characters are not human—for example, when they are animals, spirits, organizations, or features of the physical environment, such as storms—they still behave mostly like humans. The story they enact accordingly often conveys credit or blame.

When humans began creating stories, they fashioned one of their great social inventions. In our complex world, causes and effects always join in complicated ways. Simultaneous causation, incremental effects, environmental effects, mistakes, unintended consequences, and feedback make physical, biological, and social processes the devil's own work—or the Lord's—to explain in detail (Tilly 1996). Stories exclude these inconvenient complications. Novelist Margaret Atwood shrewdly marks the difference between experiences and the stories we tell about experiences:

> When you are in the middle of a story it isn't a story at all, but only a confusion; a dark roaring, a blindness, a wreckage of shattered glass and splintered wood; like a house in a whirlwind, or else a boat crushed by the icebergs or swept over the rapids, and all aboard powerless to stop it. It's only afterwards that it becomes anything like a story after all. When you are telling it, to yourself or to someone else. (Atwood 1997: 298)

Even when they convey truths, stories enormously simplify the processes involved. They single out a small number of actors, actions, causes, and effects for easy understanding, and articulate far better with assignments of responsibility than do ordinary scientific explanations. They easily break into smaller packets: simple combinations of subject, verb, and (sometimes) object:

ANTOINETTE RUNS

or

SAM HITS FELICITY

That elementary structure makes it easy to recombine the information within stories many different ways, or to single out just one packet for close examination (Franzosi 2004). As a teacher, I rely on stories day in, day out. They make it possible to teach one element or connection at a time rather than presenting the whole confusing mess at once. Whether true or not, they ease human communication.

Aristotle's *Poetics* presented one of the West's first great analyses of stories. Speaking of tragedy, which he singled out as the noblest form of creative writing, Aristotle described the two versions of a proper plot:

> Plots are either simple or complex, since the actions they represent are naturally of this twofold description. The action, proceeding in the way defined, as one continuous whole, I call simple, when the change in the hero's fortunes takes place without Peripety or Discovery; and complex, when it involves one or the other, or both. These should each of them arise out of the structure of the Plot itself, so as to be the consequence, necessary or probable, of the antecedents. There is a great difference between a thing happening *propter hoc* and *post hoc*. (McKeon 1941: 1465)

A "peripety," for Aristotle, was a complete reversal of a state, as when the messenger who comes to comfort Oedipus actually reveals to him the identities of his father and mother. A "discovery" was a fateful change from ignorance to knowledge, an awful or wonderful recognition of something previously concealed; in the story of Oedipus, a discovery (the messenger's announcement) produced a peripety (Oedipus's unmasking as a man who killed his father and bedded his mother). Aristotle caught the genius of the story: one or a few actors, a limited number of actions that cause further actions through altered states of awareness, continuity in space and time, an overall structure leading to some outcome or lesson.

By attributing their main effects to specific actors (even when those actors are unseen and/or divine), stories follow common rules of individual responsibility: X did it, and therefore deserves the praise or blame for what happened as a result. Their dramatic structure separates them from conventions. In fact, they more closely resemble classic dramas. They generally maintain unity of time and place instead of jumping among temporal and geographic settings. They involve limited casts of characters whose visible actions cause all the subsequent actions and their major effects. They often have a moral.

Let us not imagine stories as nothing but heavy-handed sermons. They can bring good news or bad news, provide amusement, bond children with their parents, and educate. I used to enjoy telling what I regarded as whimsical stories to my four children, and now persist in trying similar stories on *their* children; at least the storytelling grandfather gets some pleasure from the interchange.

Bag-snagger Ian Frazier provides a beautiful specimen of a light-hearted story. He explains how he and friends began retrieving plastic bags they found stuck in the higher limbs of city trees. Although he makes his living as a widely admired writer, he starts an account of his avocation as a snagger of bags like this:

> For more than ten years now, I've been tangled up with the problem of plastic bags stuck in trees. If I've learned anything from the experience, it's "Be careful what you notice." I was living in Brooklyn; I noticed the many plastic bags flapping by their handles from the high branches of trees, cheerful and confident and out of reach. Noticing led to pondering, pondering led to an invention: the bag snagger, a prong-and-hook

device that, when attached to a long pole, removes bags and other debris from trees with satisfying efficiency. My friend Tim McClelland made the first working model in his jewelry studio on Broome Street, downtown. Possessing the tool, we of course had to use it; we immediately set off on a harvest festival of bag snagging. (Frazier 2004: 60)

Frazier's essay goes to tell how he, Tim McClelland, and Tim's brother Bill began traveling New York City, then the whole United States, snagging bags and other debris from trees across the country, while getting cooperation from officials and environmental activists in many places. But that first paragraph does it all: provides an answer to the question "How did you ever get into bag snagging?" The answer runs:

noticing → pondering → inventing → producing → using

It even conveys a kind of moral: perceived necessity is the mother of invention.

Conventions, as we have seen, do yeoman service in confirming and repairing social relations as well as in rationalizing practices. But stories take on work of their own: integrating the puzzling, unexpected, dramatic, problematic, or exemplary into everyday life. Fiction and drama center on stories, but so do biography, autobiography, news reporting, sermons, speeches, and a wide range of conversations. Just as competent human beings become skilled at supplying conventions that conform to the social situation and at challenging reasons that fail to fit the conventions, growing up human involves learning to construct stories for a wide range of circumstances.

Credible stories likewise vary from one relationship and practice to another: telling your audience why you suddenly lost your train of thought in the midst of a speech differs from telling your best friend. "Sorry, I lost my place," might do for the audience, while "I noticed that red-headed woman in the second row looking upset at what I was saying," might be necessary for the friend.

As with conventions, effective stories vary greatly in character with the equality or inequality, distance or intimacy of the relation between giver and receiver. Plausible stories generally require more elaboration and self-justification when offered by inferiors to superiors than when offered by superiors to inferiors. Equal partners more frequently insert explicit confirmations of mutual respect and understanding into their stories. At the distant end of the distant-intimate range, both parties typically impose stringent limits on the length and complexity of the explanations they exchange, while at the intimate end detailed explanations not only occur regularly but also frequently lead to further reflections and reassurances regarding the relationship.

The Work of Stories

Try a simple exercise. Choose two settings where you often spend time. Avoid settings in which people regularly use codes or technical accounts, such as courtrooms and laboratories. Waiting rooms, commuter trains, coffee bars, and staff lounges will serve you well. Note what happens when people talk about events that are puzzling, unexpected, dramatic, problematic, or exemplary. Compare what you observe in the two settings. I am betting that your notebook will reveal these features of everyday explanations:

- People will usually tell stories to explain the events in question; they won't settle for general principles ("Pride goeth before a fall") or conventions ("She's just unlucky"), even if they end their stories with general principles or conventions.
- The stories will have no more than a handful of characters, will include a small number of actions by those characters, will treat what

happened as effects of those actions, and will take place within a single time and place.

- Actors' dispositions (rather than, say, pure accident or fate) will cause most or all of their actions.

- Dispositions will figure even more centrally when the narrator is the central actor.

- The stories will omit a large number of likely causes, necessary conditions and, especially, competing explanations of whatever happened.

- A few master stories—A let B down and B suffered, C and D fought to a standstill, and so on—will recur, so much so that listeners will often guess what comes next.

- The stories will usually have some kind of moral, at least by assigning praise or blame to one or more of the characters.

- Questions that challengers raise will much more often concern attributions of praise, blame, or disposition ("Are you sure that's what he meant?") than the overall cause-effect structure of the story.

- The exact conventions and idioms that storytellers use, however, will differ distinctly between the settings.

In short, as it responds to events in everyday life that demand explanation, reason giving depends on the types of standardized stories that already circulate in the reason-giver's social setting.

Like conventions, stories do four different kinds of relational work: establishment of new relations, confirmation of existing relations, negotiation of contested or changing relations, and repair of damaged relations. Most often, they confirm existing relations; witness the embarrassment people often feel when they have to explain the same action simultaneously to two people with whom they have very different relations—for example, spilling the groceries all over the floor at a supermarket in the presence of one's spouse and of fellow shoppers. Stories involve negotiation, however, on such occasions as discovering that unbeknownst to either of you, your job interviewer turns out to be a college classmate. Relational repairs regularly involve stories if one friend, inadvertently or otherwise, revealed damaging information about the other friend to third parties: "How could you tell them about that?"

As with conventions, the choice of stories obviously has consequences for later relations among the parties to the stories, and typically involves justification or condemnation of certain practices. If I tell you that a mutual friend has cheated me, I am simultaneously aligning you with me against the friend and warning you not to trust the friend with money, delicate information, or responsibility in important enterprises. That is why hearing such stories often upsets us and sometimes incites us to challenge the teller; if we accept the story, we take on the consequences.

Many stories, however, have positive consequences. When American civil rights sit-ins started to spread rapidly in 1960, participants often told stories of spontaneity: all of a sudden we saw our chance, so we acted together without prior planning. Later, sociologists delighted in tracing previously existing connections among places and people who got involved in the civil rights movement (e.g., McAdam 1988, Morris 1984). But at the time activists insisted that they had acted on impulse. Well, not quite: impulse with some significant qualifications. Francesca Polletta not only interviewed dozens of civil rights activists but also combed contemporary discussions among activists in campus newspapers, other publications, and the files of the Student Nonviolent Coordinating Committee (SNCC). She found "spontaneity" operating within important limits.

Looked at more closely, the standard stories of the time had two recurrent features: explicitly, they centered explanations of what happened in sit-ins and related events on students and their campuses; implicitly, they asserted that we, the student civil rights activists, were coherent political actors in our own right. "In the stories that students told and retold about the sit-ins," reported Polletta,

> spontaneity denoted independence from adult leadership, urgency, local initiative, and action by moral imperative rather than bureaucratic planning. Narratives of the sit-ins, told by many tellers, in more and less public settings, and in which spontaneity was a central theme, described student activists and potential activists to themselves and, in the process, helped to create the collective identity on behalf of which students took high-risk action. Sit-in stories—and their narrative form was crucial— also motivated action by their *failure* to specify the mechanisms of mobilization. Their *ambiguity* about agents and agency, not their clarity, successfully engaged listeners. (Polletta 1998a: 138; see also Polletta 1998b, 2002, 2005; Polletta and Jasper 2001)

"Ambiguity" does not quite capture what happened in the stories: the narratives left out such crucial actors as civil rights organizations, teachers, and churches, along with their interventions and effects. For all their neglect of relevant agents, actions, and causes, furthermore, the stories did not lack agents: "we" stood at the action's center. "Our" efforts produced its major outcomes. Inside and outside of social movements, stories about how "we" acted together repeatedly combine the two aspects: laying claim to credit for creditable accomplishments, and asserting the existence of a credible actor that deserves attention (Abell 2004, Tilly 2003a). Stories simplify actors, actions, causes, and effects. Their rationales gain clarity through simplification.

Stories as Rhetoric

So far I have simplified my own explanations of stories by writing as though their producers were speaking monologues in solitude to unresponsive television cameras. The solo image conceals the fact that stories always occur as parts of conversations, and other people often intervene in the telling. Even in the extreme case when (like Jerry Falwell's radio and television followers of the *Old-Time Gospel Hour*) the audience remains unseen and distant, the speaker operates on a theory of the audience's likely response. Here Aristotle can help us again. This time, Aristotle's *Rhetoric* comes in handy. For Aristotle, dialectic combines logical propositions with induction from rigorous evidence in an effort to prove a case beyond doubt. Rhetoric parallels dialectic, but combines arguments with examples in an effort to persuade. Neither one amounts to science, which for Aristotle requires irrefutable establishment of general principles.

Aristotelian rhetoric comes in three varieties:

POLITICAL: arguing for or against a proposed course of action

FORENSIC: attacking or defending someone

CEREMONIAL: praising or condemning someone

In all three varieties, effective rhetoric depends not only on solid logic but also on canny knowledge of human character and emotion. It depends on relations among speaker, arguments, and audience. Aristotle proposed an inescapably relational account of rhetoric.

As his discussion drew to a close, Aristotle drew on his knowledge of audiences to offer rhetoricians sage advice:

As to jests. These are supposed to be of some service in controversy. Gorgias said that you should kill your opponents' earnestness with jesting and their jesting with earnestness; in which he was right. Jests have been classified in the *Poetics*. Some are becoming to a gentleman, others are not; see that you choose such as become *you*. Irony better befits a gentleman than buffoonery; the ironical man jokes to amuse himself, the buffoon to amuse other people.

> The Epilogue has four parts. You must (1) make the audience well-disposed toward yourself and ill-disposed toward your opponent, (2) magnify or minimize the leading facts, (3) excite the required state of emotion in your hearers, and (4) refresh their memories. (McKeon 1941: 1449–50)

Two conclusions follow directly. First, a rhetorical effort's success depends on how well the rhetorician gauges the reaction that today's audience will give to the combination of speaker and arguments. Second, the same arguments and speakers will have different effects on different audiences. Both lead to the same injunction: know your audience, and watch its reaction.

Since he addressed his *Rhetoric* to the Greek city-state's equivalent of the televangelist—the public orator—Aristotle did not make a third point that probably would have been obvious to him. In the *Politics*, he insisted on the intrinsically social nature of human beings. Taking Aristotle one step farther, we should notice that most rhetorical work takes place in the course not of one-sided oration but of two-sided conversation. What is more, the other conversationalists commonly intervene in the argument to anticipate, confirm, or challenge where it is going. The skilled rhetorician, in her turn, checks continuously to see how the other participants are taking the story she is telling.

Journalists learn to be rhetoricians par excellence. In the guise of objective reporting, they engage in the business of persuasion. They often reinforce their own stories by referring to authorities as backup for explanations they have already formed. They do so, I think, because mention of the journalist's authorities, to adopt Aristotle's terms, makes the audience well-disposed toward the journalist's story and ill-disposed toward her opponents, magnifies or minimizes the leading facts, excites the required state of emotion in listeners or readers, and refreshes their memories. Journalist Alexandra Kitty argues that reference to authorities (a) lends an air of factuality to a story, (b) validates inside information, (c) compensates for the fact that journalists can't be everywhere, and/or (d) fulfills the obligation of journalists to convey official information. Appealing to authority, remarks Kitty,

> may lend precisely an air of factuality to a news story. In covering a bank robbery, eyewitness accounts may be compelling, but they may also be partial or otherwise inaccurate. A district attorney or a law enforcement agent discussing the event gives the story far greater weight. Customer complaints about fraudulent business practices are less compelling than such charges issued by a government agency. An ordinary citizen has far less credibility than someone who carries a title. (Kitty 2003: 349)

Although I'm not much of an authority, now and then journalists call me to check some matter about which they are writing. When journalists ask me about stories they are writing, they rarely ask for facts. Most often, they try to get a quotable bit that will reinforce the point they already want to make. They ask for rhetorical assistance.

We rarely think of physicians as rhetoricians. Yet physicians also draw repeatedly on rhetoric, especially when they have bad news to convey. The manual for medical interviews I quoted in chapter 1 offers insight into how rhetorically skilled physicians check their audiences. The manual calls one process "education about illness":

> There are six steps in the process of educating a patient about his or her illness: (1) eliciting the patient's ideas about etiology; (2) providing a basic diagnosis; (3) responding to the patient's feelings about the diagnosis; (4) checking the patient's knowledge of the illness; (5) providing details of the diagnosis; and (6) checking the patient's understanding of the problem. (Cole and Bird 2000: 36)

The process describes a conversation. The physician who initiates it does not simply announce a scientific opinion ex cathedra. She converses with the patient, persuading the patient to accept a story and the course of action that follows from it.

In that process, physicians often have to deliver bad news. When skilled doctors deliver bad news, they gauge its recipients carefully. That often involves letting the recipients fill in the blanks before pronouncing the fateful word. Quoting earlier work by Hackett and Weisman, Douglas Maynard provides this compelling example:

> A woman who complained to her doctor about headaches and was told it was her "nerves" asked why was she nervous. [The doctor] returned the question. She replied, "I am nervous because I have lost 60 pounds in a year, the Priest comes to see me twice a week, which he never did before, and my mother-in-law is nicer to me even though I am meaner to her. Wouldn't this make you nervous?" There was a pause. Then the doctor said, "You mean you think you are dying?" She said, "I do." He said, "You are." Then she smiled and said, "Well, I've finally broken the sound barrier; someone's finally told me the truth." (Maynard 2003: 16–17)

Who did the better rhetorical work in this conversation, to be sure, remains open to interpretation. But that is the point: the brief story—you are dying, and your imminent death accounts for some surprising changes in the behavior of others around you—emerges from a delicate conversation, not from a monologue.

Excuses, Apologies, and Condemnations

Even routine stories often carry a moral edge of praise or blame for self and others. But excuses, apologies, and condemnations loom especially large in stories when at least one of the parties is trying to renegotiate or repair the relationship between the parties. When I arrive forty minutes late for lunch with an old friend, if he's still waiting I owe him more than the New Yorker's conventional reason, "the subway was a mess." My story repairs the damage my tardiness has done to him and our friendship. But if the same old friend has recently betrayed my confidence by telling a third party some embarrassing news about me, I may well tell a different story: I was so mad that I almost didn't come at all, but finally decided to have the matter out with him; in that case, we are renegotiating our relationship, perhaps even ending it.

While pursuing quite a different set of questions, Po Bronson has collected a marvelous set of stories, often coupled with excuses, apologies, and condemnations. During the 1990s, Bronson published two novels and a nonfiction book about Silicon Valley, all best sellers. He then started thinking about changing direction, and channeled his personal career concerns into a new book. He called his book *What Should I Do with My Life?* The book mostly tells stories of people who make abrupt, dramatic changes in their work. In an intensely personal style, it also chronicles Bronson's search for the people, reports his conversations and outings with them, and includes a number of people who failed to make the shifts they longed for, as well as one engineer who stuck contentedly with his calling. As Bronson says,

> I didn't know that I would meet so many wonderful people. I never expected how honest they would be with me. I didn't know that I would learn so much from them. I didn't know that this book would become a vehicle for me to express a new voice. I didn't know that my desire for this book would survive my son's birth, or the catastrophe of September 11, or our parents' falling ill. All that unfolded for me later, like a reward for trusting my instincts. (Bronson 2002: 362)

We see Bronson thrusting himself into other people's lives, sometimes telling those people that they are deluding themselves, examining their lives for insight into fulfilling, productive matches between people and their work, eliciting story after story. The stories have a double interest for our purposes, since the storytellers usually highlighted relations between themselves and other important figures in their lives, but were also negotiating their relationship to Bronson, the insistent interviewer and friend-in-the-making.

Carl Kurlander, for example, had been doing premed classes at Duke when a short story he wrote catapulted him into Hollywood as screenplay writer for the film *St. Elmo's Fire*. During the filming, he went out with star Andie McDowell. He promised her "that when the shooting wrapped he was moving home to Pittsburgh, where he had grown up, to write short stories about their generation, stories from the heart, something deep, something real" (Bronson 2002: 131). He didn't, at least not for a long while. Kurlander heard about Bronson's book project and contacted him, in part to warn him against the seductions of Hollywood success to which he, Kurlander, had succumbed. He had gained money and recognition by writing a teenage sitcom, *Saved by the Bell*. He declared himself disgusted with his self-betrayal. "By most people's measure," comments Bronson, "he was a success—he was well off, and he was well known in his industry. But by his own measure, Carl had turned his back on his purpose in life" (Bronson 2002: 131).

Then, to Bronson's surprise, Kurlander actually took a one-year appointment at the University of Pittsburgh. Bronson made a trip to Pittsburgh for a new conversation with Kurlander and to attend a lecture Kurlander was giving to students and faculty in the university's film studies program. Afterward, according to Bronson's report,

> When we reached the car, I asked, "Aren't you afraid you're going to swap Hollywood's voice for Academia's voice? The Three-Act Structure replaced by the Freytag Triangle? Trying to impress lesbian erotic poets rather than studio executives?"

He paused, and took his response in a different direction. "See, how can you do that? Somehow you cannot idolize a place like this. How come I can't? You've been here one day, and you can see into the shadows better than I do after three months."

"I just don't want you to lose track of why you came here."

"God, I wish I had your sincerity. Really. You're like Gary Cooper."

"Don't idolize *me* now."

Another pause. "How do I do it?" he asked.

"Not lose track?"

"Yes."

"Don't live for their approval. Don't live for anyone's approval."

"Everyone wants approval."

"That's just argumentative."

"They do!"

"Sure they do. But you can take a break from it. Not forever, but a while." (Bronson 2002: 134)

In this conversation and others with Kurlander that Bronson reports, we watch two professional storytellers negotiating their relationship with each other and with others, as they explain themselves, frequently making excuses, apologies, and condemnations. Stories become the vehicle by which they create, confirm, repair, and recast the connection between them.

Telling Life Stories

As Po Bronson's book illustrates, by its very nature storytelling often involves biography, recounting at least a piece of a life story. Full biographies typically include multiple stories, one per episode, and sometimes culminate into a grand story. They, too, simplify actors, actions, causes, and effects. No doubt that is one reason why, along with self-help books, biographies so regularly head bestseller lists:

they follow a recognizable, accessible mode of explanation (Plummer 2001). They tell stories.

To be sure, biographies can take the form of codes, as in the exemplary lives of saints. They can also become technical accounts, as psychological or medical specialists try to decipher the secrets of a Julius Caesar or a Woodrow Wilson. Daniel Bertaux and Catherine Delcroix have turned what they call "family case histories" into a systematic tool of social history, a special sort of technical account. At Quebec's Laval University, they asked their students to pick a person of student age who had lived two or three generations earlier, trace that person's family connections back to all his or her grandparents, then forward to the person's descendants and her or his siblings' descendants. Public records such as birth, marriage, and death registers supplied significant shares of the evidence, but the students had to fill in from a wide variety of other sources, including interviews. Bertaux, Delcroix, and their students retold the family history as they captured one small fragment of Quebec's history.

Starting with sixty students and their chosen historical reference individuals, the exercise brought back impressive evidence about social change in the province:

> Taken together, these sixty family case histories mapped out many aspects of social-historical change as it had taken place in this region of the Quebec province for the past seventy years. In older generations one could find a vast majority of small farmers, and even one trapper (*coureur des bois*) having married the daughter of an Indian chief. In the next generation, farmers had mostly disappeared, being replaced by workers in the building trades, in industry and urban services, both in Quebec and in the north-east of the United States: family sizes got much smaller, married women who had a job were much more numerous. In the third generation the occupations in teaching, social work, health

services were fast growing. But what was most fascinating were the details of this vast collective history: how social historical change had *actually* taken place, through diverse, local, contingent mediations and initiatives, endeavours, dramas, victories, circumstances and happenstances—
some happy, some tragic. (Bertaux and Delcroix 2000: 72–73)

Bertaux, Delcroix, and their students had discovered a device that
inserted stories into a systematic analysis of social change: a catalog
of many, many events concatenating into a story no single one of the
events could tell (Tilly 2002a).

It can even work for autobiography. Autobiographical codes occupy a small, special niche as they take the form of résumés, job interviews, campaign speeches, and applications for membership in hon-
orary societies. Self-written technical accounts occupy an even
smaller space, but they also exist. Occasionally, for example, sociologists ask other sociologists to write autobiographies that include analyses of the social processes that produced, or at least channeled, their
lives (e.g., Berger 1990, Riley 1988). Even there, the urge to defend
oneself by means of stories wells up. As sociological autobiographer
Irving Louis Horowitz remarks, autobiography is "a tactic for making
people take seriously the words and deeds of their leaders, an ar-
resting presentation of self." Autobiography, Horowitz continues,
"provides a role model for the behavior of others and, at the same
time, reveals one either to be an exemplar of moral behavior to be
emulated or, the reverse, an exemplar of immoral behavior and hence
of pitfalls to avoid in one's own life" (Horowitz 1977–1978: 173; for
Horowitz's own dramatic story of his Harlem childhood, see Horowitz 1990). As a result, in fact, most sociologists do a poor job of
turning their own lives into objects of sociological explanation. They
have a strong tendency to normalize themselves, to make themselves
representative members of categories (Tilly 1993).

My personal favorite in turning a profession's gaze on itself does not come from sociology, but from history. Somewhere around 1980, indefatigable intellectual organizer Pierre Nora persuaded seven of France's most prominent historians to take themselves as historical objects. Here, said Nora, "historians try to make themselves their own historians" (Nora 1987: 5). In *Essais d'égo-histoire* (Essays in Self-History), he somehow inveigled famous French historians Maurice Agulhon, Pierre Chaunu, Georges Duby, Raoul Girardet, Jacques Le Goff, Michelle Perrot, and René Rémond to study themselves in historical magnifying mirrors. Chaunu, for example, began his historian's self-analysis by declaring "I am a historian because I am the son of *la morte* [the dead woman] and the mystery of time has haunted me since childhood" (Nora 1987: 61). Chaunu's mother had died when he was nine months old. He did not learn until much later that the mysterious "woman in white" he saw in the family photographs was *la morte*, his absent mother. He portrays his career as a lifelong effort to unravel the mysteries of absent time.

Not all the authors provided so much personal detail. "For a long time," began Georges Duby,

> in fact, right up to the moment of starting my final text, my plan was to write in the third person in order to keep my distance. I gave up the plan for fear of looking pretentious. Let me make a major point at once: I am not telling my life story. We have agreed that in this ego-history I will only display part of myself: the ego-worker, or perhaps the ego-artisan. Because I say nothing of painting, for example, of theater or music, because I say nothing of the ones I love, obviously the essence of my life remains silent. (Nora 1987: 109–10)

Having known, or at least having met, all the authors during my own career as a French historian, I found myself combining the roles of critic, historian, and peeping tom as I read the essays, peering through well-framed windows into creative lives by means of their authors' stories. Autobiography as a kind of technical account almost always veers toward stories, with their simplified actors, actions, cause-effect relations, and morals.

Autobiography, whether written or oral, usually strings together a number of stories into what may simply remain as so many stories but occasionally concatenates into a vast story: an *apologia pro vita sua*. Consider the subversive contributions of British Communist historian Raphael Samuel to the genre. Except for occasional reminiscences of his own experience in left-wing politics plus one pungent (and characteristically unfinished) essay on his very urban family's relation to the countryside, Samuel never wrote a formal autobiography. But almost everything he wrote relied on autobiography; his personal reflections and observations intertwined with critical interpretations of social history, mostly British, in which he was a major player for three decades.

Samuel received a diagnosis of cancer in April 1995, and died of it only twenty months later, in December 1996. He left behind masses of notes and incomplete manuscripts, some of which historians Sally Alexander and Gareth Stedman Jones collaborated with Samuel's (nonhistorian) widow, Alison Light, to assemble into a magnificent collection called *Island Stories: Unravelling Britain* (Samuel 1998). Samuel and his editors bequeathed lovers of English history a volume for repeated browsing rather than straight-through reading. The browsing gives a strong sense of Samuel's life and works. The book overflows with stories galore, interlarded with subtle autobiography. A reader closes the book delighted with Samuel's aperçus, tantalized by ideas briefly flashed upon the screen and then erased, tempted to scrawl questions, challenges, or exclamations in the margins, and astonished by all that learning. The reader hears Samuel's impassioned voice.

Samuel was a great initiator of historical inquiries. He was also an intellectual packrat. On separate sheets of paper he filed quotations, précis, notes, clippings, photocopies, and odd thoughts for later re-shuffling into the raw materials of his writing. The writing shows it: adorned with footnotes, stuffed with quotations and allusions, often packing so many ideas into a single sentence that it begins to sag under the weight:

> On the other hand 'British' is a term which is currently enjoying a small vogue, partly, it may be, because it is less loaded than English with cultural baggage, and therefore less exposed to the heritage-baiters, but also because, in current post-colonial usage as in the older imperial one, it is multi-ethnic and therefore more able to acknowledge the emergence of a multi-faith, multi-cultural society. (Samuel 1998: 49)

As the sentence indicates, Samuel often elbowed his enemies (here both merchants and critics of the heritage industry) on his way through the crowd. He also wrote with vivid if acerbic wit, as in a passage just three lines above the one just quoted: "The teaching of English literature is associated with the missionary position in sexuality, parochialism in high politics and tea-shop gentility in the world of letters." A lot of his stories substituted down-to-earth accounts for other people's highfalutin theories.

We read Samuel's pages less for argument than for insight, less for theory or even narrative than for context and connection. In the provision of historical insight, context, and connection, Samuel had few peers. Responding to Linda Colley's attribution of unifying force to Britain's militant Protestantism, for example, Samuel not only reviews many moments since 1536 when Protestants have divided with other Britons or among themselves, but also quotes Haslam Mills on the aunt who "challenged by a sentry, would have said not 'English,' certainly not 'British' but 'Methodist.' " Samuel's stories most often attribute historical action to distinctive states of mind.

Autobiography of a Thug

Raphael Samuel's most sustained contribution to autobiography characteristically concerned not his own life, but someone else's. Between 1973 and 1979, Samuel repeatedly interviewed former London thug Arthur Harding, who was eighty-seven years old when the interviews began. In the preface to his edition of Harding's oral history, Samuel declares: "These *Chapters* have been drawn from tape-recorded reminiscences taken over a six-year period. The story of how they came to be constructed—and the battle of wills entailed in the making of them—is contained in a companion volume (*East End Underworld: South-West Bethnal Green*), to which the interested reader is referred" (Samuel 1981: viii). So far as I can determine, the companion volume never appeared in print: par for the Samuel course! But the book Samuel advertised as "volume 2" of the set contains a sensational series of autobiographical reports. They illuminate the early twentieth-century world of petty crime in London, and connect it to the everyday lives of poor people. Despite an unending parade of colorful incidents and personalities, most reports feature one or a few actors, a limited number of actions that cause further actions through altered states of awareness, continuity in space and time, an overall structure leading to some outcome or lesson. They qualify as stories.

Born in 1886, Harding grew up in the poorest sections of London's generally low-income East End. His father, a hard drinker who rarely worked, soon abandoned his family except to ask for an occasional handout. Crippled by a runaway milk wagon when a recent bride, his mother also drank heavily until Arthur grew big and tough enough to intimidate the local bartenders. But throughout her life she took up work in their shabbily furnished room or rooms to help support her four children. Nevertheless, Arthur received most of the nurture that came to him as a child from his sister Harriet (Mighty), four years older than he. The enterprising Mighty herself carried on a remarkable series of retail businesses, some of which also put her on the wrong side of the law. Eventually, she and her mother made most of their income from dubiously legal high-interest money lending.

From ages nine to twelve, Arthur lived mostly in Dr. Barnardo's orphanage, but then he returned to the East End streets. The young Harding spent much of his time on the streets, and much of his street time in illegal pursuits such as picking pockets and van-dragging—stealing from the backs of delivery vans. He also became something of a street brawler and enforcer who sometimes got involved in protection rackets. For years, most of Harding's income came from illegal activities. He spent ten years (1911–1916 and 1917–1922) in prison for major crimes. Over his criminal career, he went to court as a defendant thirty-two times and won discharge or acquittal twenty-seven times. He was a rough customer. But by the time Samuel started taking down his life history, Harding had been out of jail almost fifty years. His autobiographical reflections on a criminal career looked back seven decades.

Harding's autobiographical stories actually described other people more often than himself. Repeatedly he placed an acquaintance in a category, assigned a character to him or her, then told a small story. In a passage about Jewish criminals with whom he had worked, for example, Harding recalled:

> Another was Jackie Shinebohm. He was a very clever pickpocket—so nice-looking that nobody suspected him. He was fourteen or fifteen when we first met up. I picked him up round the coffee stall at the top of Bethnal Green Road. I said to him 'What are you at?' and he said, 'I'm a whizzer' (pickpocket). So I knew you could trust him and he was clean. He had no parents or nothing—sometimes he used to sleep at my place in Gibraltar Gardens. Jackie got killed in Ireland in 1922. He was there with a gang of pickpockets, four or five of them. They'd got the

police straightened up so that they wouldn't interfere with their business, and he was talking to a couple of Dublin CID chaps and it seems the Sinn Feiners spotted him and put a tail on him. They followed him to the hotel where he was staying and shot him dead. It was just an honest mistake. They thought he was a spy. (Samuel 1981: 77)

During his late teens, Harding began to go off with some companions on pickpocketing "expeditions" through England and Wales. Remembering a Welsh expedition, Harding noted that "Jewish people were the safest people to stop with. They had bad memories of the police in Russia and weren't fond of giving them information. You could trust them because they had a verb in Yiddish 'Thou shalt not'—they were not supposed to injure another person. Jewish people were very homely, they did not seem to mind that I was a 'Yok' " (Samuel 1981: 78). So the stories roll on: actor(s), character, action, consequences, and often a moral conclusion.

But Harding himself evolved across his stories. He soon added armed robbery to his portfolio, specializing in stickups at illegal gambling parlors, where the Jewish patrons were unlikely to call in the police. By that time, nevertheless, the London police had a full record on him, and watched him closely. "In 1908," he recalled,

I was sentenced to twelve months imprisonment under the Prevention of Crimes Act. I hadn't done anything at all. I was put away as a suspected person. When I came out I was much more vicious in my behavior. People avoided me like the plague. The police began to give me a wide berth. I started to beat up many of the villains who were regarded as 'terrors'. I was now in the prime of my life and according to the police I was the terror of Brick Lane. I was noted for always carrying a gun and that was the cause of my being famous, but I didn't have to use any weapon to make myself feared. If we'd wanted money we could have made a fortune—everybody in Brick Lane was scared of us. But money wasn't a great influence on me. If my mother and sister was all right, that was enough. (Samuel 1981: 117–18)

Around the age of twenty-five, Harding switched from picking pockets to "snide-pitching": changing false money. It was safer than pickpocketing, he said, because if you knew the law you could often get off even when caught with a bad coin (Samuel 1981: 80). His sister, Mighty, would mail counterfeit coins to the town where he and his gang were planning to work, and where they would pass the coins for purchases and change in local shops. Harding had some close calls with the police in the course of his snide-pitching career, but he served his major prison terms for other offenses: participating in an armed attack on the gang of a pimp who was competing with another pimp that asked Harding to help him, and passing stolen money.

In the first case, by his report, Harding's collaborators got him into serious trouble not by overdoing the armed attack but by bringing firearms into court after their beaten opponents had sworn out complaints against them. In the second case, his mother had actually received the money from the robber, who deposited it in the Christmas Club she and her daughter were running. Although Harding, according to his claim, did not know that the depositor had stolen the large bills, he suspected they were hot, and paid them out to people he thought he could trust. When the Bank of England came after a pub owner who had taken a five-pound note, the publican fingered Harding. By that time (1916), Harding's arm-long criminal record weighed against him. Despite a debatable indictment, he eventually went back to prison for five years.

That ended his criminal career. Married in 1924 and soon a father, Harding had another brush with the law for fighting in 1926, but got off and never went to jail again. And the moral of this story? Over six years of interviewing, Harding took more than one strong position. But the overall structure of the story that emerges from the edited tapes runs something like this: a young man emerges strong from enormous hardship, makes his way as best he can considering local conditions, always defends his family (except perhaps his father), repeatedly gets raw deals from the authorities, but recognizes the increasing cost of criminal associates along with the declining returns of criminal activity, marries a good woman, and becomes a law-abiding citizen. In the long run, character tells.

Stories of Sickness

Even stories of sickness can be uplifting if properly told. Alison Light reports, in fact, that Raphael Samuel wrote almost half of his *Island Stories* during his all-too-brief cancer treatment (Samuel 1998: xii). But others have made serious illness itself the subject of their stories. Take the editor, critic, essayist, and fiction writer Anatole Broyard. Broyard's final book shared some properties with Samuel's posthumous volume. In the course of a long writing career, Broyard had published powerful essays on his father's final illness and on the literature of death. Broyard received a diagnosis of metastatic prostate cancer in 1989, and immediately went into treatment, only to die fourteen months later.

Soon after his diagnosis, Broyard started writing an extraordinary book about his experience of cancer and its treatment. He completed three essays and a set of journal notes. They appeared in 1992 (along with two of the earlier essays and an epilogue by his widow, the psychotherapist Alexandra Broyard) as *Intoxicated by My Illness, and Other Writings on Life and Death*. In a foreword, Oliver Sacks remarks that

I have never seen any writing about illness that is more forthright—nothing is glossed over, or evaded, or sentimentalized, or pietized—and that is at the same time deeper, more intelligent, more reflective and resonant. You feel the man himself—who is also and always a critic and an artist—seize his pen with unprecedented force, determined to challenge his illness, to go into the very jaws of death, fully alive, pen in hand, a reporter, an analyst, to the last. He takes his pen almost to the darkness. His final journal notes go to within a few days of his death. (Broyard 1992: xii)

Clearly, Broyard wrote more than a straightforward story; he wrote a prose poem about sickness, death, and dying. But because his personal experience focused his thought, the book contains some of the most compelling stories on the subject I have read.

Here is a Broyard passage that will resonate with many a sick person:

When my father died, I tried to write a novel about it, but I found that my whole novel was written politely. I was so pious about death that it was intolerable, and I find that people are doing that to me now. They're treating me with such circumspection. They're being so nice to me. I don't know whether they really mean what they say or whether they're accommodating me. It's as though they're talking to a child, and I want them to stop that. I can't find them anymore. I need their help, but not in this form. The therapist Erving Polster defined embarrassment as a radiance that doesn't know what to do with itself. We need a book that will teach the sick man's family and friends, the people who live with him, what to do with that radiance. If they knew how to use it, their radiance might do him more good than radiation. (Broyard 1992: 22–23)

Broyard was then, of course, writing the very book about which he was writing: a book that showed how to find radiance in sickness. In this sophisticated passage, nevertheless, we discover a powerful story with Aristotelian overtones: people are treating me tenderly because they fear hurting me. Doing so, they are hurting me.

But Broyard also searched for nontechnical explanations of his own condition. Like many sick people, he recounted what might have caused his malady—and therefore what he might have done differently to avoid it:

> My first reaction to having cancer was lyrical—irony comes later. It's part of the treatment. While I don't know whether this is lyrical, ironical, or both, I'm tempted to single out particular women and particular practices that strike me now as more likely to be carcinogenic than others. Coitus interruptus, which was widely practiced before the Pill, seems a likely suspect, and oral sex comes to mind as putting a greater strain on the prostate. But after saying this, I want to make it clear that I certainly don't hold my cancer against these women—whatever I did, it was worth it. I have no complaints in that direction. I wouldn't change a thing, even if I had known what was coming. and though this is only a fantasy, this talk of femmes fatales and pleasure you can die of, it's part of the picture of the cancer patient, and I don't want to edit out anything that belongs to my case. (Broyard 1992: 26)

As he went on, nevertheless, Broyard wove an artful story: of fatal illness as a creative opportunity.

Although most of us do not write about the passage into illness so lyrically as Anatole Broyard, he certainly did not invent the idea of disease as a new world containing its own distinctive challenges. Douglas Maynard illustrates the sense of crossing a threshold at the onset of illness:

> This movement from one to another world is captured in the remarks of a physician who was diagnosed with a cancer in his right leg (synovial sarcoma). Appearing in a Public Broadcasting System program called "When Doctors Get Cancer," he is shown walking on crutches into a hospital and, with a baseball cap covering a bald head, sitting on a bed

while undergoing chemotherapy and being examined. The doctor is now a patient, and in a voiceover, he says, "Back in October, a year ago, I was given six months to live. So here I am today, a year later, with a new world, a continuum of my last one but essentially a new world." That bad news can usher one into a "new world" is vividly captured not only in this statement but in the picture of this doctor now in patient garb and in the patient role. (Maynard 2003: 11)

Broyard probably would have rejected the PBS broadcast's optimistic spin. But he could certainly have told the cancer-stricken doctor about crossing a brilliant threshold. Reading Broyard's book, writer and prostate cancer victim Robert Vaughn Young confided to his own journal "I had found someone whose words expressed my excitement and explained why my priorities had shifted" (Young 2001: 6). Stories may do mundane work, but they need not be uninspiring.

One of my daughters, the molecular geneticist Kit Tilly, gave me a copy of *Intoxicated by My Illness* shortly after the book's publication. On an accompanying postcard depicting a Greek monastery, she wrote the note "I hope you don't find this to be morbid. I found it to be fascinating." She knew that a few years before I had survived a melanoma, and would therefore inevitably compare my experience with Broyard's. What neither she nor I could then know was that over the next dozen years my equivalents of Broyard's doctors would detect metastasized prostate cancer in my system before twice discovering and treating lymphomas. As a souvenir from my own period of utter baldness brought on by chemotherapy, I have saved a wig I never dared wear.

Having quite forgotten the Broyard book on my biography shelf, I wrote a book of my own—not about illness, but about the history of social movements—to focus life and hope during the treatment for lymphoma (Tilly 2004a). I call it my cancer book. Apparently rid

of the lymphomas but still harboring stubborn, invisible, metastasized prostate cancer cells in some nonprostate corner of my body, I
now re-read Broyard with heightened pleasure, pain, relief, and a
twinge of guilt: he died, but I survived. To my illness-sharpened eyes,
Broyard's stories set a chastening standard for creativity in the face
of death.

My own lugubrious stories run the risk of distracting you from
their main point. Stories do social work. They not only help account
for puzzling, unexpected, dramatic, problematic, or exemplary
events, but also help confirm, redefine, or challenge social relations.
Their element of rhetoric—always relating speaker to audience—
should make that clear. But their frequent reliance on socially available templates, their interpretation as signals concerning relations
between givers and receivers, and their sometimes powerful effects
on self-esteem reinforce the point. Perhaps one last example will help
nail it down. For a book on the downward mobility of middle-class
Americans during the 1980s, anthropologist-sociologist Katherine
Newman interviewed more than 150 once-affluent people at length
about the experience of falling from comfortable circumstances to
the impoverished margins of their former lives.

Newman begins her book with the story of David Patterson (whom
we first encountered in chapter 1), an electronics executive recently
transferred from California to New York who lost his job and his job
prospects when his hard-hit firm closed the division he was heading.
Patterson had a lot to lose: brought up in a Philadelphia working-class
slum, the first member of his family to attend college, he had been the
whole family's pride and joy, owner of a big house and two luxury cars,
supporter of a wife and two children who had adapted comfortably to
an affluent style of life. And now he couldn't find a job.

Newman chronicles Patterson's move from one story to another.
So long as his hopes of transferring his executive skills to a new job

held up, he clung to a tale of business as business, of market logic as inexorable, and of his firm's problems as the chances you take in a volatile industry. Eventually the focus of his story shifted:

> But after months of insecurity, depression, and shaking fear, the economic causes of his personal problems began to fade from view. All David could think about was, What is wrong with me? Why doesn't anyone call me? What have I done wrong? He would spend hours bent over his desk, rubbing his forehead, puffing on his pipe, examining his innermost character, wondering whether this or that personality flaw was holding him back. Could people tell that he was anxious? Were people avoiding him on the street because they couldn't stand to come face to face with desperation? Was he offending potential employers, coming on too strong? With failure closing in from all directions the answer came back "It must be me." The ups and downs of the computer industry and the national economy were forgotten. David's character took center stage as the villain in his own downfall. (Newman 1988: 6–7)

Once again someone else's story resonates with my own experience. My father, the child of poor German immigrants, dropped out of high school to support the family when his father suffered a crippling injury at work in a Chicago area tractor factory. While holding menial jobs, Dad took night courses, finished a high school diploma, pushed on to study accounting, and fought his way into the lower levels of white-collar work. When the Depression struck in 1929, he was working as assistant credit manager of a large Chicago camera company—nothing like David Patterson's division headship, but a significant step more prosperous than his crippled farmer-worker father, my grandfather. Dad soon lost that job as the company shrank.

My own clear memories only begin a few years later. But those Depression times brought my father—and thus the whole family— long periods of unemployment, repeated spells of temporary or part-time employment, and multiple changes of dwelling including a family sojourn in my mother's father's basement. (My maternal grandfather, who had immigrated from the strike-stilled coal mines of Wales with his five daughters and second wife during the 1920s, had fortunately kept his job as chief mechanic of the Chicago-area Ovaltine factory despite the economic collapse. We drank a lot of Ovaltine during the Depression.)

Hardship, frustration, and humiliation spilled out into the children—eventually we were five siblings—as we wore hand-me-down clothing, ate government-issue cornmeal, gathered dandelions for salad, and scrambled for whatever part-time jobs we could find. Collectively, we never shared David Patterson's confidence in the market's rationality or his descent into self-blame. Led by determined parents, we told ourselves a story of decent people buffeted by hard times. Yet we, too, depended on stories to organize our lives, and our relations to other lives.

Stories add up to a great human invention, comparable in their own zone—the organization of social relations—to the plow in agriculture. Like the plow, they use a simple application of force to dig deep. By their very nature, they frustrate purists: they condense complex life into simple plots with absurdly stripped-down causes and effects. They highlight the comedies, tragedies, moralities, immoralities, victories, and defeats of ordinary lives. Although they provide significantly more substance than conventions, they thumb their noses at codes and technical accounts, so much so that professional wielders of codes and technical accounts often find they must translate their messages into stories. When most people take reasons seriously, those reasons arrive in the form of stories.

CODES

The Connecticut-based Laura J. Niles Foundation, founded in 1997, "encourages and supports efforts that offer learning and economic growth opportunities for the motivated poor. Of equal importance are charitable initiatives that foster life enrichment through canine and other types of animal companionship" (Niles Foundation 2002: Home Page). The foundation has, for example, given money to Children's Village in Dobbs Ferry, New York, a residential campus for troubled boys aged five to twenty. The grant helps boys in residence to train dogs for assistance to the disabled, as well as allowing disabled people two-week training sessions in which they and their new dogs get used to each other.

Behind the foundation's ability to help people and dogs lies a vivid array of legal struggles. Laura Niles (born in 1909) and her brother Henry, two years younger, inherited great wealth from their parents. For years, Laura and Henry split their time between New York City and the family estate in Brightwaters, Long Island. Laura never married, but she maintained an active social life, rode horses, played tennis, and became well known as a breeder of show dogs, especially miniature poodles. According to the foundation's website, "She was a loquacious woman and enjoyed verbally jousting with people. She was known to be both amusing and entertaining. Although she was a woman of means, she chose to live modestly" (Niles Foundation 2002: Biography). In 1986, Laura (now aged 77) moved from Brightwaters to her Blairstown, New Jersey, farm, where she raised horses as well as dogs.

At seventy-five, Henry Niles was declining in physical and mental health. When Laura moved, he stayed behind on the Brightwaters estate. Serena Bono, about thirty years younger than Henry, began caring for him. By 1990, Henry had lost the ability to manage his own life and finances. Geoffrey Parkinson, the Niles's Long Island neighbor, family friend, and investment counselor, then intervened to have Joseph Kunzeman, a former judge, appointed as Henry's conservator and himself appointed financial advisor. Meanwhile, Serena and Henry started a romance. Despite a restraining order obtained by Parkinson and Kunzeman, Serena and Henry actually married in 1992.

About the same time, Laura established three trusts to endow the future Laura J. Niles Foundation with the bulk of her estate; Parkinson served as trustee. But Laura (now eighty-three) soon began spending more time with Henry, Serena, and Serena's son, Salvatore Bono. Among other things, she bought a $700,000 condominium the four of them occupied in Naples, Florida. In 1997, she also revised her will, replacing Parkinson with Salvatore Bono as executor and trustee. That same year, Henry died. Until then, Salvatore had been collecting rents for a landlord and pizzeria owner while trying unsuccessfully to set himself up as an insurance broker. The new will included large amounts of money for the Bono family. Salvatore became a full-time manager—or pillager—of Laura's finances, spending money freely on himself and his family.

After sixteen months of Salvatore's extravagance, Parkinson filed suit, claiming his fees as former trustee, asking further fees for his financial advice, and requesting a court-appointed guardian for Laura. He justified the request for a guardian on the legal ground of *undue influence*: the claim that recent in-laws Serena and Salvatore had improperly used their personal sway over Laura to alter her will and loot her estate. A New Jersey court complied, appointing a lawyer as guardian and initiating a trial of the Bonos on the civil charge of undue influence. About the same time, Laura lapsed into a coma from which she did not recover before dying.

The law of undue influence intertwines with testamentary law. In general, courts require of a valid will that the testator understands: (1) the nature and extent of his/her property; (2) the "natural objects of his or her bounty"—who would ordinarily have justified claims on the estate; and (3) the terms of the will she or he is signing. For undue influence, the court must find that the alleged influencer had motive and opportunity, as well as actually intervening to shape the outcome. Neither a bequest to an unexpected recipient nor exclusion of a "natural object of bounty" suffices to establish undue influence.

Despite the fact that siblings sometimes accuse each other of undue influence over their parents' wills, American case law generally presumes that close relatives and household members "naturally" influence each other. Hence such accusations face stiffer legal tests than claims of undue influence by relative outsiders, such as lawyers, doctors, employees, friends, and recently acquired lovers. If these outsiders occupied what the law calls a "confidential relationship" with the testator and benefited significantly from the will, courts entertain complaints of undue influence much more readily.

Confidential relationships (also known as fiduciary relationships) include those outside of close kinship that give at least one party great power to influence another party's decisions. In cases of major bequests to persons in confidential or fiduciary relationships, goes the legal principle, the burden of proof for legal propriety shifts from other parties to the will's beneficiary, who must refute the presumption of undue influence.

Judges typically scrutinize stories offered by plaintiffs and defendants in undue influence cases, but then match the elements of those stories that they accept with categories and precedents available in case law. Even their judgments of motives usually depend as much

on analogies with what other people would do in the same circumstances as on direct evidence concerning states of mind. The matching produces reasons based on codes rather than new cause-effect
accounts. It adopts formulas, not explanations. Unlike the formulas
of conventions, as the law of undue influence demonstrates, the formulas of codes depend for their interpretation and application on
extensive technical knowledge. Law school teaches people how to
acquire that knowledge: how to identify and interpret relevant stat-
utes, what previously decided cases provide citable precedents, what
sorts of evidence the applicable formulas require.

For cases of undue influence, three New Jersey estate lawyers
sum up:

> A variety of factual scenarios demonstrate how an undue influence claim
> might be supported. The most extreme example of undue influence is
> the use of physical coercion. This could be as blatant as physically forc-
> ing the signing of a will by holding a gun to the testator's head or with-
> holding basic life necessities, such as food and medical treatment, from
> a testator until the will is signed.
>
> However, undue influence claims usually surface in a less extreme
> manner:
> - when there are unexplained changes in the manner in which the testa-
>   tor disposes of the property under a new will;
> - circumstances involving "unnatural" or "unjust" gifts;
> - when there is a heightened susceptibility of the testator being influ-
>   enced;
> - when the testator's financial and business affairs are controlled by the
>   influencer; and
> - when the length of the relationship between the testator and the
>   alleged influencer is questioned, such as when the testator becomes
>   involved with a new paramour. (Fishkind, Kole and Mannion
>   2003: 2)

In the case of Laura and Henry Niles, all these conditions applied in one way or another. They led the New Jersey courts to credit all three elements of the test for undue influence: motive, opportunity, and effective intervention. On behalf of the Niles Foundation and of Parkinson's claims on the Niles's estate, Geoffrey Parkinson's attorneys persuaded several New Jersey courts to nullify Niles' revised 1997 will and to force substantial repayments of money taken from Laura Niles's estate—and therefore indirectly from the foundation—by Serena and Salvatore Bono. The repayments included legal fees incurred by Parkinson and the Laura J. Niles Foundation. Two justices of the New Jersey Supreme Court dissented from the ruling on fees, citing the American Rule against charging defendants who lose a suit with the plaintiff's legal fees.

The majority, however, declared that in this case of egregious undue influence, the defendants' behavior justified an exception to the American Rule. The majority opinion included this passage:

> In this appeal a mother and her son working as a team unduly influenced an eighty-eight-year-old, single, demented multimillionairess to modify three inter vivos trust agreements to name the son as trustee and to confer upon them substantial economic benefits under the altered trust agreements. The former trustee and the primary residuary beneficiary under the former trust agreements successfully prosecuted litigation to remove the illegitimate trustee and to require the mother-son team to make the estate whole except for certain counsel fees. The issue raised in this appeal is whether to create an exception, if one does not exist already, to the American Rule, which generally does not permit a prevailing party to recover counsel fees from a losing party. We hold that when, as in this case, an executor or trustee reaps a substantial economic or financial benefit from undue influence, the fiduciary may be assessed counsel fees incurred by plaintiffs and third parties in litigation to re-

store the estate's assets to what they would have been had the undue influence not occurred. We also hold that the mother-son team should be jointly and severally liable for all reasonable counsel fees authorized by this opinion. (Niles Case 2002: 4)

We may well suspect the New Jersey Supreme Court's majority of taking satisfaction from meting out justice to the Bonos. But their justification for bending the American Rule did not center on mother-son dishonesty. It stressed financial gain the Bonos had made from their manipulation of the trusts.

Cases of undue influence often involve intense family dramas: siblings or children who elbow each other on the way to an inheritance, newcomers who take advantage of feeble oldsters, long-time companions who find themselves cut out by greedy relatives. They almost always raise questions of fairness. But in their legal deliberations on undue influence, courts downplay questions of fairness in favor of well-established procedural rules. When they offer explanations of their rulings, as in the Niles case, they do not propose cause-effect stories or technical accounts, much less conventions. Instead, they offer codes. The three tests for a valid will and the three further tests for undue influence convert the stories given by witnesses, plaintiffs, and defendants into matches between legal principles and what courts accept as the facts of the case. Those matches become code-based justifications for the court's decisions. They follow formulas. In the legal melting pot, conventions, stories, and technical accounts all give way to codes.

How Codes Work

Reasons based on conventions draw on widely available formulas to explain or justify actions, but include little or no cause-effect reasoning. Story-based reasons, in contrast, build on simplified cause-effect accounts by means of idioms that many people in the same culture can grasp. Reasons stemming from technical accounts likewise invoke cause and effect, but rely on specialized disciplines and claim to present comprehensive explanations. When it comes to codes, reasons given for actions cite their conformity to specialized sets of categories, procedures for ordering evidence, and rules of interpretation. Together, categories, procedures, and rules make up codes.

In addition to justifying reasons, codes serve a variety of purposes. The codes that linguists simplify and standardize as grammars make communication possible among speakers, writers, and readers of the same language. At any historical moment, painting, music, poetry, and other public arts conform to codes that make artists' productions intelligible, but also allow their audiences to recognize creative innovations. Solemn rituals, civic or religious, provide occasions for confirmation of shared commitments. None of these uses for codes necessarily involves the giving of reasons.

Codes figure in the world of social analysis as well. Economic and political analysts who call themselves "institutionalists" stand out from their brethren by their insistence that implicit and explicit codes provide essential underpinnings for markets, electoral systems, and other complex structures.[1] Even the World Bank, once a bastion of the idea that markets regulate themselves, has started to talk of "building institutions for markets" (World Bank 2002). Codes covering contracts, property rights, official transparency, and bankers' obligations to depositors all occupy important positions in the infrastructure the Bank hopes to promote in developing countries. They lead to checklists—formulas—according to which experts can rate countries that vary in their approximation to an ideally institutionalized market. Checklists state the rules.

[1] See, e.g., Besley and Case 2003; Campbell 2004; Feige 1997; Kogut 1997; Lieberman 2002; North 1997; Scott 1995; Stinchcombe 1997.

Codes have their own dynamics. Categories change, procedures for ordering relevant evidence change, interpretive rules change, and the three interact. Most visibly, participants change the rules. We most easily detect a code when we discover a connected set of rules for behavior in some arena of human activity—the law, of course, but also some other arena of professional expertise, a complex game, or a specific organization. Within any such arena, authorities commonly change the rules as they encounter some new problem; accumulated rules therefore provide a map of significant earlier problems people have faced in their arena.

James March, Martin Schulz, and Xueguang Zhou have looked closely at alterations in the academic and administrative rules of Stanford University from 1891 (the university's founding) to 1987. They break the near-century into "rule regimes," marking a new regime when a major change in the procedure for making rules occurred; 1968, for example, brings a new regime for administrative rules because during that turbulent year the university installed a faculty senate. (Having spent the 1968–69 academic year at Stanford, I still re member that festival of debates and demonstrations.)

Within each rule regime, the Stanford researchers find a declining rate of innovation in rules as time goes on. Their finding suggests a two-phase process: first a shakedown, as people discover discrepancies, gaps, and bad fits within the new regime; then a long phase of settling in as people within the organization gradually find ways of reconciling their own programs to the rules, and the rules to their own programs. Changes of rules in one area, however, continue to stimulate changes in adjacent areas of the organization. Changes of rules governing undergraduate majors, for example, have a good chance of requiring further changes of rules concerning graduation credits.

External influences also matter. In the case of Stanford, governmental intervention made a difference in rules, with academic rules accelerating when governmental intervention increases, but *adminis-trative* rules showing the opposite effect:

> The greater the increase in the proportion of higher education revenues coming from the federal government, the fewer the new administrative rules and the fewer the administrative rule revisions. The effects of federal pressures on rules may well depend on the involvement of the federal government in the funding of universities, but the creation of new administrative rules at Stanford is more associated with periods of declining funding than with periods of increasing funding. It appears to be the tightening of funds that focuses attention on administrative procedures. (March, Shulz, and Zhou 2000: 167)

After living through several cycles of university belt-tightening, I can readily believe that rules change and proliferate when financial crisis strikes; suddenly who pays for photocopies and who gets free telephone service become issues. The same sort of reasoning applies to codes of professional conduct, religious codes, educational program requirements, grammars, and bureaucratic practices; far from simply expressing abstract principles, codes emerge from the give and take of organizational life. They therefore contain residues of organizational histories and limit current behavior within organizations.

Here, however, we zero in on a narrower question: how specialized codes—of whatever contents, however they develop, and whatever other purposes they serve—provide the basis for the giving of reasons. Asked to justify a decision, adjudicate a dispute, or give advice, skillful users of codes find matches between concrete cases and categories, procedures, and rules already built into the codes. Like conventions, reasons based on codes therefore gain credibility from criteria of appropriateness rather than from the cause-effect validity that prevails in stories and technical accounts. In the case of legal codes, whatever cause-effect reasoning participants may apply to the case at hand, the matching of evidence concerning behavior to available legal

categories prevails. As lawyer, professor, and judge John T. Noonan
sums it up, "Rules, not persons, are the ordinary subject matter of
legal study" (Noonan 2002: 6). Legal specialists ask into what category the behavior falls, whether the participants in the case (including
lawyers, judges, and juries) have followed acceptable procedures, and
what legally established rules apply.

Formulas in Operation

Another New Jersey undue influence case dramatizes that logic of
appropriateness. Anna Villone Catelli was a childless widow who
lived alone. Her brother Robert Villone died in 1994, leaving the
bulk of his estate to their nephew Thomas Villone, a self-employed
long-distance truck driver who lived in Arizona. Thomas called Anna
to report her brother's death. Before then, she and Thomas had
rarely seen each other. Now, Anna asked Thomas to visit her the next
time he came to New Jersey. He started visiting regularly.

Anna held a major interest in the family firm Excelsior Realty
Ltd.; another nephew, George Villone, served as Excelsior's general
partner. As of early 1994, Anna went to her attorney and signed a
will leaving bequests to relatives, friends, and two churches, with
the remainder going to her physician and confidant Dr. Coppola.
She also gave Thomas her alternate power of attorney in case Dr.
Coppola was unable to serve. But the 1994 will simply made
Thomas one of multiple beneficiaries, along with George. During
that year, Anna suffered a major stroke that left her paralyzed, with
greatly impaired speech and sight. Dr. Coppola, who had her power
of attorney, moved her into the Garden Terrace Nursing Home.
Thomas continued to visit her at Garden Terrace on his trips from
Arizona to New Jersey.

In November 1995, Dr. Coppola called Thomas in Arizona to tell
him that Anna had decided to make Thomas her sole heir. Three

days later, Dr. Coppola died. Dr. Coppola's son turned over the estate papers to Thomas. In Arizona, Thomas hired a lawyer who wrote up a living trust and a will naming him as executor and sole heir. The Arizona attorney instructed Thomas (who had a high school education, and no legal background except as his uncle's executor) to have the documents reviewed by a New Jersey lawyer, and recommended that Anna hire her own lawyer to represent her interest. Instead, Thomas drove to New Jersey in January 1996, went straight to the nursing home, and spent three days reading the documents to Anna.

By this time, Anna had too little sight to read for herself, and had suffered general impairment:

> The nursing administrator who saw her daily conceded that, while she had made progress in recovering from her stroke, her level of functioning was seriously diminished. Her short-term memory was significantly impaired. Her vision had deteriorated substantially. She required total care by the staff at the nursing home, needing daily assistance with feeding, bathing, and other basic needs. During the three days prior to the execution of the document, she did not leave her room, but remained in bed, dozing from time to time and barely communicating with anyone. (Catelli Case: 3)

On the third day of reading aloud, Thomas had Anna place an X on the will's signature line and arranged for the nursing home administrator to witness and notarize the signature.

Anna lived until the next year, 1997. But as soon as Thomas had her signature, he went into action. He gave up truckdriving and appointed himself full-time administrator of the trust. Almost immediately, he issued $30,000 in checks from the trust to himself and his family. He soon sued to take Anna's interest in Excelsior Realty from George Villone. George resisted. After Anna's death, Thomas sued both to force a transfer of the Excelsior interest to him and for admission of the 1996 will to probate. George filed an objection. Spurred by George's objection, judges began to rule that Thomas had exercised undue influence over the 1996 execution of the living trust and will.

The successive New Jersey courts that examined the case certainly reconstructed the story of Anna, Thomas, George, and Dr. Coppola. They unquestionably made assessments of cause and effect, especially in judging how Thomas had produced such a favorable outcome for himself. But the legal proceedings did not pivot on what happened or why. They focused instead on the formula for a valid will, especially the requirement that the testator understand what she is signing. They singled out the appropriate category (competent testator), procedures for processing evidence (proper recording of testator's intentions), and interpretive rules (means of establishing both competence and influence).

The courts decided that Anna, too blind to read the documents Thomas presented to her, could not have understood them. The New Jersey courts' legal rulings emphasized three points: (1) the confidential relationship between Thomas and Anna, which shifted the burden of proof from George to him; (2) the combination of Anna's inability to read the documents with the absence of a third party who could testify that she had understood and assented to their contents; and (3) Thomas's failure to recruit an attorney for representation of Anna's interest. They invalidated Anna's 1996 will, the one Thomas had read to her.

The rulings had a surprising implication. They indicated that if Thomas had actually met the legal requirements in the second and third regards, Anna's 1996 decision to make Thomas her sole heir might well have been legally valid. After all, Anna's brother had earlier willed the bulk of his estate to Thomas, apparently without contest. Dr. Coppola had actually communicated Anna's decision in a telephone call he made shortly before his own death. Although a story concerning how and why Anna affixed an X to her revised will in January 1996 appeared prominently in the case's legal record, the court's decision did not center on the truth or falsehood of that cause-effect story. In short, the rulings translated materials from stories into codes. They penalized Thomas for the mismatch between his behavior and the law.

By definition, legal disputes activate codes. In such disputes, pleas and decisions typically stress correspondences between legally established facts and available principles rather than cause-effect explanations. Categories, procedures, and invoked rules all sometimes call up challenges. Claims of error sometimes challenge alleged facts, but more often concern misapplication or neglect of available principles. These features of legal disputes matter for our purposes because they clarify distinctions between disagreements based on codes and other sorts of disagreements.

Conventions smooth interpersonal relations without relying on expert knowledge. Disputes about conventions generally center on what they imply for the relationship between givers and receivers of reasons, rather than how elegantly they fit available protocols. Stories open up the field to competing explanations, but employ idioms that many people share. Disagreements between technical accounts resemble codes in requiring learned expertise, but rely less on logics of appropriateness than on competing claims of what causes what. (As the next chapter shows, however, technical disputes sometimes feature disagreement about measurement practices and instruments; such disagreements shift the question toward codes.) The wide employment of codes in medical practice will clarify these distinctions.

Medical Codes

We have already watched medical personnel giving reasons in the form of conventions, stories, and technical accounts. But we have not yet noticed how regularly codes play parts in medicine. Human health and illness involve such complexity that no nurse, physician, or technician could possibly provide a complete explanation of any patient's current condition. Medical codes reduce that complexity in several different ways. They:

1. catalog symptoms so that practitioners can sort people's problems into likely underlying conditions, most often defined as diseases or injuries
2. provide standardized vocabularies into which practitioners can translate patients' observable conditions, and with which they can communicate their interpretations of those conditions to other specialists
3. set up appropriate matches between diagnoses and treatments, often summarized in manuals and textbooks
4. in a synthesis of the first three, set the standard of good practice against which teachers of medicine judge their clinical students, review committees judge hospitals, and courts adjudicate claims of malpractice

Although a skilled physician always knows things about particular patients, maladies, and cures that dictate deviations from available codes, a great deal of medical practice consists of matching remedies with conditions according to established codes (Bosk 1980; Timmermans and Berg 1997). Into what category does this patient fall? Given such a category, how should medical personnel collect, process, and record evidence about the patient's condition? Given category and evidence, what treatments apply?

Codes have long pervaded medical education. For many years, sociologist Aaron Cicourel worked with hospital medical teams, observing closely how they actually got their work done. Cicourel reports the following dialogue from the 1970s between a female Training Fellow (TF) and a male Attending Physician (AP) in the rheumatology service of a university hospital:

TF: OK, next is Elena Louis, she's 44 years old and sent here from oncology. So, for two years she's been having episodes initially of erythema followed by swelling in the second and third metacarpals and the

PIP joints of both hands, first one and then the other. She also had arthritis in her ankles, with a red spot on the exterior of the lateral malleolus followed by swelling. First came the red spot, then pain and swelling within 24 hours. That lasted for a few days, and then went away. But while it lasted, the pain was very sharp. It greatly limited her use of her hand as well as her walking. Mm, she doesn't actually complain very much about her joints except for some stiffness in her back and other joints. She didn't really have any problems with her elbow or her shoulders. Uh, she doesn't have any nodules. She doesn't have Raynaud, doesn't have Sjogrens. She's always tired. She's starting to have a lot of cramps in her legs. Uh, there's no history of arthritis in her family. She has no occasional morning sickness, but it's not real . . .

AP: How long has this been a problem?

TF: Two years. She saw a Dr. Blumberg at St. Miguel, and they told her she had degenerative joint disease. Before that, she saw another doctor who told her that she had rheumatoid arthritis. At some point, they put her on tolectin, but she didn't think it did her any good, and now she isn't receiving any medication . . . uh.

AP: No organic illness, right?

TF: Right. But back then she weighed 380 pounds and, um, now she's lost 200 pounds. She had an intestinal blockage at Riverdale around 1970 . . .

AP: She had a real live intestinal blockage?

TF: That's what she said. (Cicourel 2002: 108–9; my translation checked against Cicourel 1984)

What's going on here? As Cicourel analyzes the situation, the Training Fellow is trying to place the patient within a classification of rheumatic disorders including these categories:

- rheumatoid arthritis
- osteoarthritis

- rheumatoid variants
- systemic erythematic lupus
- gouty arthritis

Each of these categories has a standard clinical description, to which the Training Fellow must match what she knows of the patient at hand. Her report implicitly rules out rheumatoid arthritis, rheumatoid variants, lupus, and gouty arthritis in favor of osteoarthritis. In fact, the supervisor later told Cicourel, the Training Fellow had misdiagnosed as osteoarthritis what further investigation revealed to be rheumatoid arthritis (Cicourel 2002: 112–13). We watch a fledgling physician, with her supervisor's help, learning how to perform a double conversion: from observation, interview, and physical examination of the patient into recognizable symptoms, then from symptoms to a standard diagnosis. A later step (which Cicourel's story doesn't show us) matches treatments to diagnoses. The process matches facts to codes.

Like university rules, medical codes change as a result of problems encountered using existing codes. Scientific and clinical research also produces modifications in codes. To any twenty-first century rheumatologist, the 1970s code adopted by the hospital where Cicourel made his observations looks antique. Current classifications of arthritis distinguish fibromyalgia, osteonecrosis, osteoporosis, Paget's Disease, Behcet's Disease, Lyme Disease, and other conditions absent from the 1970s roster, while excluding osteoarthritis entirely. But physicians' matching of observations to symptoms and symptoms to established codes continues to dominate the path leading from complaint to treatment.

American medicine long dramatized its relation to codes by means of the hospital routine called Grand Rounds. In early versions of Grand Rounds, leading physicians of a hospital service took their juniors around from ward to ward, stopped to examine "interesting" patients, offered or asked opinions on diagnosis and treatment, and used the occasion to teach appropriate matching of observations, case information, diagnosis, and treatment. Grand rounds often ended in a general conference of the touring group in which they discussed the cases they had seen, sometimes even bringing in a patient for another interview. During my time at Boston Psycho half a century ago, I occasionally sat in on the end-of-rounds conference.

Less Grand Rounds still occur in many hospitals, with a service's attending physician, residents, interns, and medical students discussing patients currently under treatment in the service. A manual on rounds for attending physicians and residents describes a conference room exchange among the attending physician (Dr. Goff), the resident (Al), and a student (Susan):

> After Susan completed her presentation of a patient with substantial respiratory problems, Dr. Goff asked, "Looking over the list, what do you think she might have?"
>
> "Sarcoid?" responded Susan questioningly.
>
> "Sarcoid!" What does sarcoid have going for it?" Goff quickly asked.
>
> "Well, it's a restrictive type of disease," came Susan's reply.
>
> "What percent of sarcoids don't exhibit a problem x-ray?" followed Goff.
>
> Susan sat there stumped, so Al, the resident, chimed in, "Thirty percent."
>
> "Therefore a chest X-ray is important because seventy percent of sarcoids have a problem," Goff said emphatically. (Weinholtz and Edwards 1992: 46–47)

A significant share of clinical teaching occurs in rounds-based conferences of this sort. Once again, the attending physician is teaching the student to match clinical observations with diagnosis, which will lead to a further match of diagnosis with appropriate treatment.

Over recent decades, nevertheless, the decline of open wards, increased protections for patient privacy, and complications of diagnostic technology have all pushed Grand Rounds toward something much more like a medical school forum: speakers, presentations, discussions, sometimes pharmaceutical industry sponsorship to publicize a new drug (Burton and Roth 1999). In the Internet age, Grand Rounds have mutated into online presentations of cases for worldwide distribution. Baylor College of Medicine, for example, regularly broadcasts cases electronically (Richardson 2002). In a 2002 presentation of a thyroiditis case, Baylor physicians included questions for online discussion, each one followed by "click here for answer":

1. What is the differential diagnosis of the neck pain and tenderness in this patient?
2. What is the differential diagnosis of the suppressed TSH and elevated T4?
3. What are potential treatment options based on the differential diagnosis?
4. What are additional differential diagnoses at this time?
5. What tests may aid in establishing the diagnosis? (Case and Balasubramanyam 2002: 2, 4)

Even in their contemporary forms, Grand Rounds center on matching clinical observations with codes for diagnosis and treatment.

Since the 1970s of Cicourel's observations, American physicians have felt greatly increased pressure to make their code-matching visible, public, and standardized (Rothman 1991). In reaction to intervention by lawyers, ethicists, insurers, hospital administrators, and health management organizations, physicians have invented an approach called "evidence-based medicine":

Using evidence-based medicine in clinical practice requires some changes in physician behavior. For years, clinical decision making was based, primarily, on physician knowledge base and expert opinion. Accountabiity was centered on patient outcomes, with success determined by meeting the agreed-upon treatment goals, rather than having accountability rest with the healthcare insurance companies. State medical boards provided the "final" accountability, if a patient brought legal action. Now physicians are expected to create, maintain, and improve on standards of care that have measurable outcomes and can be applied with a high degree of quality control and accountability. Increased patient sophistication, brought about, largely, by mass media coverage of medical advances and information accessibility on the Internet, and globalization require that physicians provide evidence validating the treatments or testing procedures they choose. Soaring medical costs have prompted healthcare insurance companies to establish formularies and treatment guidelines that further affect physicians' choices. (Nierengarten 2001: 2)

Evidence-based medicine does not necessarily cure illnesses or save lives (Berwick 2003). It does, however, give public conformity to established codes even more prominence in contemporary medical practice than it occupied in earlier medical training.

Medical Malpractice

Suits charging medical malpractice cast a stark light on medical codes. When something goes seriously wrong during or after medical treatment, patients or their families often sue the responsible doctor or institution. A website for lawyers begins its examples of "strong cases" for medical malpractice suits with a frightening alphabetical roster of untoward medical incidents:

Anesthesia

A patient underwent surgery with Halothane (fluothane) as the anesthetic agent, even though he had suffered previous biliary tract disease, which made the use of this anesthetic contraindicated. The patient died as a result of liver necrosis due to the effects of the anesthetic.

A trainee anesthesiologist ran out of oxygen before the operation was completed, causing the patient to suffer a fatal cardiac arrest.

A patient who underwent surgery for the repair of a pilonoidal cyst under epidural anesthesia ended up with uncontrolled movement of the lower extremities.

Angiography

A patient underwent angiography (dye study of the arteries). The procedure was improperly performed, and the patient suffered brain damage.

Burn Treatment

A patient suffering from severe third-degree burns received inadequate and improper "burn therapy."

Childbirth

A child was born with a blood problem—Rh incompatibility—antibodies developed by the mother were destroying the blood in the baby. The attending physicians and hospital personnel failed to detect the child's condition. (Lawcopedia 2004: 1)

The alphabetical listing continues on from horror to horror. If any of these events happened to you, me, or our next of kin, we might very well sue the doctor or the hospital.

When such cases reach juries and the juries decide in the plaintiff's favor, the same juries often make large awards. In 2002, St. Mary's

Hospital of Brooklyn and Dr. Randahir Bajaj appealed a 2001 jury award of $144,869,495 to Michelle McCord. The *New York Law Journal* reported the judgment as the year's largest medical malpractice award across the whole United States (McCord Case 2002, note 2). In 1988, McCord, who was then twenty-eight and seven and a half months pregnant, developed breathing difficulties after free-basing crack cocaine. She went to the St. Mary's emergency room. Emergency room personnel inserted a tube running from McCord's mouth through her trachea and into her lungs, feeding her oxygen through the tube. When she seemed to stabilize late the same day, the team then working at St. Mary's removed the tube under Dr. Bajaj's supervision. As they removed it, McCord's larynx closed in a spasm. The staff failed in an attempt to reinsert the tube. Although a surgeon eventually performed a tracheotomy and inserted a new oxygen tube, by that time McCord had suffered cardiac arrest and permanent brain damage.

After eight months at St. Mary's, McCord moved to the first of several long-term group care facilities, where she was still functioning at a low level when the jury finally decided her case thirteen years later. The jury assigned 75 percent of the liability for her brain damage to the hospital and 25 percent to Dr. Bajaj, who had ordered the first tube removed. The jury "found several departures by defendants from good and accepted medical practice regarding Ms. McCord." The jury award included "$383,161 in past lost earnings, $957,696 in future lost earnings over 31 years, $2 million in past medical expenses, $11,528,636 in future medical expenses over 31 years, and $30 million in past pain and suffering and $100 million in future pain and suffering also over 31 years" (McCord Case 2002: 2). The appeals court rejected St. Mary's motion for a new trial, recommended a reduction of the award to $7,032,560—137 million dollars less!—but ordered a retrial of the award if the parties did not agree on that reduction (McCord Case 2002: 7). Even at the much lower level, the award imposed a substantial malpractice penalty on hospital and physician.

Between 1999 and 2001, the median medical malpractice jury award in the United States rose from $700,000 to $1,000,000 (Insurance Information Institute 2004). During the same period, premiums for physicians' and hospitals' malpractice insurance rose significantly, probably less as a result of rising jury awards than of overall declines in the profitability of malpractice insurance companies for other reasons, including drops in their investment income (GAO 2003: 29–32). In fact, by that time the bulk of malpractice insurance did not come from commercial firms but from physician-owned mutuals and self-insurance by large medical establishments (GAO 2003: 38–39). As premiums rose, nevertheless, trial lawyers, insurers, organized physicians, and legislators began a public round of mutual recriminations. Some commercial insurers withdrew from malpractice insurance, some medical organizations demanded controls over malpractice premiums, and others called for caps on court settlements. But attorneys' organizations replied that settlement caps punish victims of medical malfeasance (New Jersey State Bar Association 2003).

Despite sensational awards that grabbed headlines, however, medical malpractice remained a high-risk area of practice for lawyers. Since people who claim that malpractice has injured them or their loved ones rarely have much money of their own, attorneys most frequently take their cases on a contingency basis, agreeing to collect a third to a half of the plaintiff's final award after deducting documented costs (Lawcopedia 2004: 6). The trial lawyers were taking on long odds. In 2003, a state trial lawyers' association and several insurers consulted by U.S. General Accounting Office researchers provided the following ranges of estimates for outcomes in such suits:

Proportion of claims producing payments to the plaintiff (i.e., the
alleged victim of malpractice): 14–50 percent

Proportion of claims actually reaching trial: 5–7 percent

Of all trials, proportion decided in favor of defendants (i.e., physicians
and/or hospitals): 70–86 percent (GAO 2003: 23)

According to these figures, only about one case in sixteen (5 to 7
percent) went to trial, and plaintiffs won only 14 to 30 percent of
those trials, which means that something like 1 or 2 percent of all
cases filed ended in a plaintiff's victory. A reasonable guess might
therefore be that a trial attorney who took on an apparently "strong
case" as described by the lawyers' website still had only one chance
in three of collecting, with that chance depending mainly on the defendants' willingness to settle before going to trial.

As medical malpractice cases have proliferated in the United
States, they have assumed a standard form. Both legal teams seek
out—and hire—visibly qualified physicians. The expert physicians
agree to testify on one or more of three issues: (1) what standards
of medical or hospital practice prevail in this area of diagnosis and
treatment, (2) whether the physician or hospital violated those standards, and (3) whether such a violation caused the alleged damage to
the patient. Although the third item raises questions of cause and
effect, testimony and dispute generally pivot on the first two. On
those two items, physicians are testifying about codes and the
matches between performances and those codes. Did the medical
professionals place the patient in the right category? Did they properly collect and record evidence concerning the patient's condition?
Did they follow appropriate treatment rules?

Evidence-based medicine formed partly in response to just such
uses of standard codes. But its existence makes public a body of doctrine against which courts measure medical performance. When cases
actually reach a jury, the judge instructs the jury to consider the facts
as the two sides' testimony have presented them, but to match those

facts with prevailing standards of medical or hospital practice in this area of diagnosis and treatment. Expert physicians on both sides testify as to accepted medical practice, but lawyers for plaintiffs and defendants regularly cite textbooks, medical publications, and previous court decisions as well. They also match performances to publicly known codes. Accordingly, physicians and hospital personnel see the zone in which they can use their own judgments about cause and effect shrinking steadily (Marjoribanks, Good, Lawthers and Peterson 1996; Rothman 1991).

Converting Stories into Codes

Legal and medical disputes occur in a rarefied world where codes prevail. Codes belong to specialists such as rabbis, lawyers, bureaucrats, umpires, and medical ethicists. Sermons, classes, PowerPoint presentations, manuals, and how-to books often present codes: briefly stated principles followed by practical applications. Their very formats separate them from everyday social interchange. Most of day-to-day social life does not center on enactment of codes. Asked to describe or explain a social episode they have witnessed or participated in, very few people ever refer to the categories, procedures, or rules of codes.

Ordinary people—including you and me when we are not practicing our specialties—package their descriptions and explanations in stories. As a consequence, some professionals specialize in collecting stories for conversion into codes. In emergency rooms, triage nurses set down records that justify provisional assignments of patients to diagnostic and treatment categories. Social workers interview welfare applicants to determine their eligibility for benefits. Priests take confessions that become the bases for penance. Police interrogators extract confessions to serve in criminal trials. We earlier watched a medical resident converting evidence from a medical interview—stories the patient told—into material for a coded diagnosis. These professionals all perform a double conversion: from cause-effect accounts into formulas, and from popular idioms into specialized discourses.

Take the police interrogation. Police who interrogate a suspect usually know the charge, have formed at least a sketchy story of how the offense occurred, but face three demanding tasks: (1) using the suspect's responses to improve their own knowledge of what happened, (2) determining whether the suspect actually committed the offense in question or some other punishable violation of the law, and (3) posing questions and challenges that will elicit responses corresponding to the major elements of the offense as defined by the relevant legal codes. The third task involves converting materials from stories into material for codes. Police interrogators match the information they collect to the categories, evidence-ordering procedures, and interpretive rules constituting codes of criminal law.

Consider the interrogation of James Martin, small-time criminal turned murderer. During the early 1990s, Santa Barbara's public defender's office recruited sociologist Jack Katz to help the defense in the punishment phase of Oklahoma-based James Martin's criminal trial. In Oklahoma, Martin had laid down an extensive record of crimes such as fraud, forgery, and petty theft. In 1991, Oklahoma local police began searching for him on new charges. Martin stole a gun from an Oklahoma trailer park where he had worked, took his wife's car without permission, and fled to join relatives in Bakersfield, California.

After quarrels with the Bakersfield Martins, James Martin traveled to Ventura, California, where he saw an attractive recreational vehicle at the beach. He pulled his gun, commandeered the vehicle, killed the sixty-eight-year-old Canadian woman who owned it, and dumped her body off a back road in a remote part of Santa Barbara County before driving the vehicle back to Bakersfield. His Bakersfield relatives told him what they had learned from police radio: police were already searching for the recreational vehicle. He abandoned the vehicle, went back to Ventura, failed in an attempt to murder a homeless man and steal his pickup truck, then traveled somehow to Las Vegas. In Las Vegas, he killed a sixty-five-year-old blind man while burglarizing the man's residence.

A little later, Martin conned a vehicle from a used car lot and started off for Texas. Approaching a U.S. Border Patrol checkpoint near the New Mexico–Texas border, he tossed out his gun. But the border police got the gun, and found a good deal of incriminating material (including a law enforcement badge) in the car. They contacted Nevada and California police, who soon tagged Martin as a suspect in the two murders. Santa Barbara County sheriff's deputies Fred Ray and Ed Skehan came to New Mexico with the assignment of questioning James Martin. Police videotaped the four-hour interrogation. During the grilling, Martin made statements that later sealed his conviction on murder charges. Repeatedly, the interrogators asked Martin for his version of what had happened in Ventura—his story—only to challenge the story Martin had just told by pointing out inconsistencies or introducing new information. As an outside expert, Katz analyzed the taped interrogation for the defense, looking for matter that might justify a lighter sentence.

The videotape records a wrenching drama. Over and over again, Martin tells a story that denies or reduces his responsibility for the Ventura and Las Vegas crimes. The deputies listen, but then bring out details to shake the story. For example, Martin initially claims that he stole an empty recreational vehicle, and uses his long record of petty crime to make that claim plausible. After Martin has committed himself to that story, his interrogators "assert that two young boys saw him in a parking lot, pushing the RV's driver into the back of the vehicle and then driving it off" (Katz 1999: 277).

Katz does a close analysis of Martin's speech and body language during this zigzag conversation, concentrating on two points at which the deputies' replies drive Martin to tears. Katz provides such marvelous detail, however, that we also learn how the police drew from Martin the admissions they needed for matching with the relevant code—more exactly, in this case, for a code-based condemnation. After the "two young boys" bit, for example, Deputy Skehan disarms Martin by remarking that "there's a big difference here between somethin' happening intentional and not," registers Martin's nodded yes, then follows with, "You did, you did take it with the lady in it, right?" Martin shifts uneasily, finally replying "Yeah" (Katz 1999: 279). The police have their first damning admission.

The crisis mounts. The interrogators now consolidate their case. Deputy Ray moves on: "Okay, we knew that. Now, the gun, the gun, the gun that you used to shoot her with is the same gun you stole in Oklahoma, isn't it?" One of the deputies simulates a gun with his fingers, points it at Martin's forehead, and reveals, "We got the gun in there." Katz sums up:

> Martin has just learned that the police have two eyewitnesses. Suddenly he also knows that they found the gun that he tossed off as he approached the border control point. To Ray's question, "Same gun, isn't it?" Martin responds, "Yeah, basically, I guess." The police push for an unqualified admission, Skehan asking, "No, isn't it?" and Ray asking "Same gun that you used to shoot her." Martin says "God," softly. His gaze still down, Martin then says, "Well, I know I'm getting, I'm getting the electric chair for this. You know." (Katz 1999: 279)

Martin alters and elaborates his story several times after that, twice starting to weep as he recasts his portrayal of what happened and what state he was in. He describes himself as drunk when he took the RV, claims for a while that a third person in the vehicle must have killed the owner, and declares that he considered killing himself with the gun as he approached the border station.

When the interrogators begin introducing new information about the failed attack on the pickup truck's owner and the killing of the Las Vegas man, Martin increasingly portrays himself as rejected, lonely, and desperate, a hapless loser who didn't know what he was doing. Step by excruciating step, the Santa Barbara sheriff's deputies draw the materials of a coded condemnation from James Martin's changing stories. Inexorably, they gather statements that prosecutors will use to place Martin in the legal category of murderer, will present as evidence of his actions, and will array along with physical exhibits and witnesses' testimony in suitable legal form. The prosecution will match their case against James Martin with the category, evidential procedures, and decision rules that apply to murder trials.

The Costs of Codes

Not every conversion of stories into codes leads to the electric chair. Job applications, survey interviews, résumés, obituaries, and citations for honors typically require either their authors or some specialist to convert accounts initially presented in story form into stylized facts to match well-established codes. A Russian visa application recently asked me to list every country I had visited during the previous ten years, with dates. I could not possibly fill out that section of the application without telling myself a whole string of stories, year by year, and substantiating the stories for myself by checking old pocket calendars I had fortunately saved. When it came to a section asking me to list every single organization to which I had ever belonged, I gave up, writing "too many to count—mostly professional." Russian bureaucrats would rather not hear my stories, but they insist on matching my foreign travels and organizational affiliations with their own templates of suspicious activity. They ask me to do the first stage of converting my chaotic life into raw material for coding. They ask for material that they can match to their own categories, their procedures for ordering evidence, and their interpretive rules.

To the extent that we outsiders organize our reasons as conventions, stories, or technical accounts, we are likely to find codes vexing. We complain, as I just have, about "those bureaucrats" who insist on complicating and distorting perfectly sensible facts and reasons. Even from inside, rebel theologians rail against traditional interpretations, rebel physicians against rules that inhibit effective personalized treatment, rebel lawyers against legal dehumanization. Consider the indictment by lawyer-philosopher-novelist Thane Rosenbaum, who teaches at Fordham Law School. "The legal system," declares Rosenbaum,

> always seem to ignore that the public has inherent expectations about the law, which conflict with the more circumscribed vision of what the law has in mind for itself. Truth is one example of this broken trust. The legal system functions quite well knowing that most cases don't end up achieving any measure of truth. In fact, trials, legal settlements, and plea bargains generally result in either silencing the truth or bastardizing it. The legal system, for its part, is satisfied with learning facts. If the facts also turn out to be true, that's a fortuity of the legal system, not an aspiration. But facts and truths are two different concepts entirely. Facts don't have to be true. They just need to be found and applied to the law. Facts are artifacts of the justice system, while truths are trademarks of the moral universe. Fact is a legal system; truth is a moral one. The legal system's notion of justice is served by merely finding legal facts without also incorporating the moral dimensions of emotional and literal truth. (Rosenbaum 2004: 16–17)

Novelist Rosenbaum later contrasts the healing power of storytelling with the crippling power of law, demanding that the law learn to heal victims of wrongs, since "they need to be able to experience what the novelist already knows, and what the injured intuitively sense: that there is no way to heal emotionally from an injury if the story goes unheard and victims are denied their moral right to testify to their own pain" (Rosenbaum 2004: 61).

In short, the logics of appropriateness that belong to codes contradict the cause-effect moral logics that belong to stories (Noonan 2002). We have seen that contrast illustrated vividly in codes of inheritance, of organizational behavior, of medical analysis, of clinical malpractice, and of crime. If we looked into ethics, pastoral theology, architectural standards, legislative procedures, or almost any arena of professional regulation, we would encounter the same gap between stories and codes. In social life, codes do very different sorts of work from stories.

Codes emerge from the incremental efforts of organizations to impose order on the ideas, resources, activities, and people that fall under their control (Scott 1998). Once in place, they strongly affect the lives of people who work for those organizations, or who cannot escape their jurisdiction. In those arenas, they shape the reasons people give for their actions as well as for their failures to act. Even when we evade or subvert them, codes matter.

TECHNICAL ACCOUNTS

War spawned the National Academy of Sciences (NAS) and its research arm, the National Research Council (NRC). During the Civil War, President Abraham Lincoln enlisted the country's scientific establishment in the Union's ultimately victorious violence against the Confederacy. "The National Academy of Sciences," according to Alex Roland, "was created during the Civil War to help the federal government deal with the avalanche of inventions and proposals that poured into Washington, many having to do with military matters" (Roland 1999: 641). In 1862, applied science had proved its value to warfare as the ironclad Union vessel Monitor defeated the Confederate ironclad Merrimac, starting a new phase in naval combat. Meanwhile, earlier inventions such as breech-loading and repeating rifles, water and land mines, the telegraph, the railroad, and the machine gun—still marvels of applied science—were transforming war on land.

Through the U.S. Navy, government scientists who had long hoped to create an American organization rivaling the French Academy of Sciences persuaded Congress to realize their dream (Bruce 1993: 204). In March 1863, Lincoln signed the congressional Act to Incorporate the National Academy of Sciences. The act declared that the Academy,

> whenever called upon by any department of the Government, investigate, examine, experiment, and report upon any subject of science or art, the actual expense of such investigations, examinations, experiments, and reports to be paid from appropriations which may be made

for the purpose, but the Academy shall receive no compensation whatever for any services to the Government of the United States. (NAS 2004: 2)

Although the first fifty members included such distinguished civilian researchers as Harvard's Swiss-born naturalist Louis Agassiz, thirteen of them came from the army and navy. As it worked out, the NAS as such contributed little to the Union's Civil War victory. The "no compensation" provision of the enabling act voiced congressional suspicion that the new academy could become a vehicle for freeloading scientists. But its establishment certified and cemented the tie between science and government.

After the Civil War, the NAS continued to serve the government in peacetime, but also became a major forum for discussions of scientific issues among the country's leading researchers. In the midst of World War I, President Woodrow Wilson asked the NAS to expand its government service by creating a temporary research agency, the National Research Council (NRC). The NRC served Wilson's war effort well. At war's end, the NRC became a permanent organization. From that time on, it served as an important clearinghouse for American science, and an influential certifier of scientific orthodoxy.

By the late twentieth century, the NAS had grown to about 1,800 members, with seventy or eighty newcomers elected each year by the existing membership to replace those who had died recently. It had also created two parallel academies: a National Academy of Engineering and an Institute of Medicine. All three worked with the NRC. The NAS published a prestigious scientific journal, the *Proceedings of the National Academy of Sciences*. Meanwhile, the NRC established committees and working groups to report on scientific issues of national concern. Sometimes government agencies solicited reports on scientific questions they were facing, including public controversies they had stirred up. Sometimes, in contrast, groups within the academies and the NRC initiated their own inquiries, and looked for governmental or foundation support to back them.

A case in point: I once belonged to an NRC Committee on Contributions of Behavioral and Social Science to the Prevention of Nuclear War. We formed the committee because we felt that American military strategists were ignoring available social science findings, and therefore neglecting social processes that could reduce the likelihood of a nuclear holocaust. We convinced several foundations that our disciplines had something serious to say on the subject. As our efforts ended each year, we often amused ourselves by invoking the old fallacy, post hoc, propter hoc: since no nuclear war had occurred that year, we declared, obviously the behavioral and social sciences had again done their work effectively. But in the meantime, we did bring together and report the best scholarship we could find on the causes and prevention of international conflict (for a sample of our activity, see Tetlock, Husbands, Jervis, Stern and Tilly 1989). The end of the Cold War, however, put us out of business; our external sponsors decided that the risk of nuclear war had diminished to the point that prevention no longer mattered, at least to them. In similar ways, topics of NRC committees and reports shifted with the interests of governmental agencies, of foundations, and of the academies at large.

The NRC kept itself running with a wide range of projects. In June 2004, for example, the National Academies website listed recent reports on:

- dampness and mold in buildings as causes of asthma and other respiratory ailments
- whether some vaccines cause autism
- likely patterns of storms during the 2004 hurricane season

- evaluation of elementary and secondary school math programs
- the quality of women's community health care

Often the reports brought current scientific knowledge to bear on subjects that had recently caused a public outcry. The Institute of Medicine's autism study, for instance, rejected vociferous claims that the vaccine preservative thimerosal and the measles-mumps-rubella vaccine might trigger the disorder. Reports also sometimes declared that insufficient evidence existed for some widely believed conclusion, or even that scientists could not currently reach agreement on the issue at hand. The dampness-and-mold study concluded that scientists had not done enough work to establish an association between mold and fatigue or psychiatric disorders, much less to show exactly *how* dampness and mold affected asthma despite statistical evidence that they did. Such reports often ended, unsurprisingly, with calls for more and better research.

NRC reports from the behavioral and social sciences—psychology, economics, anthropology, sociology, demography, political science, geography, and related disciplines—more often conceded uncertainty and disagreement than did those from the physical and natural sciences. Physical and natural scientists could rely on experiments whose equivalent in human affairs would violate ethical limits. They could chop up bacteria, induce mutations in fruit flies, and blast molecules into smithereens, then observe the effects of their interventions. Anyone who tried the equivalent with human beings would soon be dead or behind bars. Social scientists sometimes conducted innocuous experiments in the form of invented group tasks or cognitive tests. Mostly, however, they relied on close study of "quasi-experiments," such as questionnaire surveys, or "natural experiments," such as analysis of existing differences among schools, firms, or communities.

These sorts of comparison almost always left open several competing cause-effect accounts of the process under study. Social scientists were also more likely than physical and natural scientists to take up questions on which participants, observers, and policymakers disagreed heatedly, such as causes and effects of social inequality or conditions for effective democratization. As a result, NRC reports from the behavioral and social sciences frequently ended with calls for research to adjudicate among currently competing views.

The NAS *Proceedings* published technical accounts in terms that few people outside their specialized fields could understand. Such a high proportion of *Proceedings* articles assumed knowledge of esoteric problems in physics, chemistry, and biology that I gave up my own subscription after a few years of letting the journal pile up on my desk. NRC reports, in contrast, favored technical accounts building on the best science available, but written so that policymakers and educated citizens could follow their reasoning. To that end, they typically pushed the technical accounts of specialists a certain distance toward stories. They omitted some of the incremental, indirect, environmental, simultaneous, and reciprocal effects that full technical accounts had either to include or to rule out explicitly. Nevertheless, as compared with everyday discussions of global warming, public health, and the quality of education, NRC committees—including committees from the behavioral and social sciences—produced their own versions of technical accounts incorporating the current scientific consensus.

What Do Technical Accounts Do?

How do technical accounts differ from stories, conventions, and codes? By definition, they combine cause-effect explanation (rather than logics of appropriateness) with grounding in some systematic specialized discipline (rather than everyday knowledge). Nevertheless, they often articulate with specialized codes in several different ways: because codes authorize their practitioners to carry on forms of investigation barred to nonspecialists; because codes actually govern the availability of relevant evidence; and because practitioners themselves fashion codes distinguishing between proper and improper procedures. In specialized medical research, for example, stringent codes govern who can participate in dissections or the administration of drugs, others guide the preparation of case records, and still others lay out rules for ethical treatment of participants in clinical trials.

Obviously, technical accounts resemble stories, conventions, and codes in facilitating communication within some group of specialists. Because they assume shared knowledge of previously accumulated definitions, practices, and findings, they economize on references to those definitions, practices, and findings. For that very reason, outsiders often consider technical accounts impenetrable because they are so hermetic or—if the outsider thinks they are actually dealing with subjects she knows well—filled with jargon. When it comes to reason giving, however, technical accounts parallel stories, conventions, and codes by doing relational work. This time they signal relationships with possessors of esoteric knowledge: saying you're one of us to other sympathetic specialists, marking differences within the field from others with whom the author disagrees, providing introductions to the field for aspiring newcomers or clients, and establishing the author's authority vis-à-vis respectful nonspecialists. They establish, confirm, negotiate, alter, or even terminate relations between givers and receivers.

Less obviously but no less consequentially than in the cases of conventions and stories, authors of technical accounts write them differently depending on the audiences they are addressing. There they also do relational work. Communications among specialists use shorthands that simultaneously save effort and signal membership in an in-group. Outside that narrow circle, authors necessarily provide more context, and often resort to analogies that outsiders will recognize. Science writing is an art, and editors of such magazines as *Nature*, *Science*, or *Scientific American* pour plenty of effort into translation from insider talk to discourse that motivated outsiders can follow. Technical accounts, then, pose distinctive problems when it comes to communicating results to interested nonspecialists, as in NRC reports. The more pressing and controversial the topic under investigation, the more delicate the art of constructing effective technical accounts, of establishing the right relationship between authors and audiences. Let us look at some examples.

Technical Accounts of Violence

Take the question of interpersonal violence.[1] Of course violence often calls up reasons in the form of conventions ("those folks are like that"), codes ("the law forbids") or stories ("she had a rough childhood"). Chapter 3 showed us former London thug Arthur Harding offering historian Raphael Samuel a whole series of colorful stories about his criminal younger life. But interpersonal violence also engages the attention of specialists who prepare technical accounts of its origins.

In 1988 three governmental agencies asked the NRC to produce a report on the causes and prevention of violence. The National Science Foundation (NSF) wanted advice on research priorities, the National Institute of Justice asked for ideas on the reduction of violent crimes, and the Centers for Disease Control sought information on

---

[1] For recent surveys, see Barkan and Snowdon 2001; Burton 1997; González Callejo 2002a; Heitmeyer and Hagan 2003; Jackman 2002; Krug et al. 2002; Mazower 2002; Tilly 2003b.

the prevention of injuries and deaths produced by violent behavior (Reiss and Roth 1993: xi). Although NSF surely would have accepted advice on violence at all scales, requests from the other two agencies tilted the study away from war, genocide, and other large-scale processes toward individual and small-group violence. Accordingly, the NRC recruited an expert panel weighted toward criminology, law, and psychology. On its own initiative, furthermore, the panel narrowed its focus to small-scale criminal behavior in the contemporary United States. Like other panels, this one commissioned many review papers from other experts, but debated and wrote its own synthesis of current knowledge. It wrote a technical account of small-scale, criminal interpersonal violence.

The panel's choice of perspective strongly influenced its findings, explanations, and recommendations. All three emphasized individual-level processes rather than the social and cultural complexities that other analysts of violence often stress. Social conditions figure in its report primarily as precipitants of individual behavior. The report's findings dramatize what it must explain:

- In recent U.S. experience, assaults make up the majority of violent crimes.
- Despite widespread fear of anonymous street crime, most violent crimes occur between people who already know each other, often including members of the same household.
- The United States produces more violent crime per capita than other industrialized countries.
- Current U.S. violent crime rates nevertheless fall below historic peaks.
- Members of racial and ethnic minorities make up a disproportionate share of crime victims.
- Perpetrators are overwhelmingly male and disproportionately minority, but rarely violent career criminals.

- Less connection exists between violent crime and youth gangs than people commonly believe.
- Violent crime imposes substantial losses on lives, health, and property each year.
- Investigators have found little apparent effect of increasing imprisonment on violent crime rates.

Although others have often proposed broad social and cultural explanations for similar findings, the panel zeroed in on causes and effects that operate individual by individual: aggressive patterns learned in childhood, subjection to childhood sexual abuse, excessive use of alcohol and other "psychoactive" drugs, high levels of testosterone, and so on. Social processes show up in the technical account as factors that activate or facilitate individual-level causes: concentrations of poor families, local income inequality, mobility and disruption that inhibit local communities' control over their young males, access to drugs, firearms, and crime-promoting opportunities (Reiss and Roth 1993: 14).

Accordingly, the panel recommended "problem-solving initiatives" in six main areas: (1) intervening in the biological and psychosocial development of individuals' potentials for violent behavior; (2) modifying places, routines activities, and situations that promote violence; (3) maximizing the violence-reduction effects of police interventions in illegal markets; (4) modifying the roles of commodities—including firearms, alcohol, and other psychoactive drugs—in inhibiting or promoting violent events or their consequences; (5) intervening to reduce the potentials for violence in bias crimes, gang activities, and community transitions; and (6) implementing a comprehensive initiative to reduce partner assault (Reiss and Roth 1993: 22)

All of these recommendations flow from a technical account in which psychologists, lawyers, and social scientists agree on cause-effect connections of the following sort:

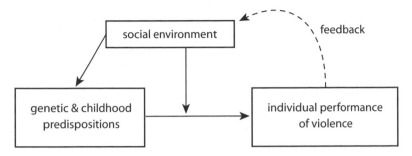

In such an account, social processes activate, inhibit, or facilitate individual behavior, but mainly mediate the relation between existing individual dispositions and actual performance of violent acts. Even this elementary technical account goes beyond everyday stories by complicating the causal chain. Most of its authors, furthermore, recognize feedback—for example, as the frequency of individual violence in a locality shapes the locality's social environment. The cause-effect reasoning illustrates how technical accounts differ from stories, and how they depend on specialized training for their plausibility. Only specialists are likely to have clear ideas of what goes into the causal arrows, and how they produce their effects.

Codes for Crime

The report's authors also veered into codes from time to time. With codes, reasons given for actions cite not their causes and effects but their conformity to specialized sets of categories, procedures for ordering evidence, and rules of interpretation. In this analysis of violence, codes show up as measurement problems. They parallel systems of medical diagnosis and bureaucratic rules. But now they take the form of "statistical information systems."

The panel's professionals drew the evidence used in their report chiefly from three statistical sources: a National Crime Survey that each year asks a national sample of persons aged twelve and over what crimes they have recently experienced; a Uniform Crime Reporting System that compiles information from police departments; and the vital statistics program of the National Center for Health Statistics, which tabulates death certificates for homicide (Reiss and Roth 1993: 2). The authors rightly pointed out that for such violent crimes as rape, child abuse, and assault, available statistics greatly understate actual levels.

The assembled experts also recognized that in these and similar cases classifications become morally, legally, and politically controversial. At what point does intimacy on a date become date rape? Do parents have the legal right to spank their children? Does induced abortion count as murder? How much discretion should police have in whether to register citizens' complaints as crimes, whether to make arrests in family disputes, and how to classify injuries in barroom brawls? These questions take the study of criminal violence out of cause-effect territory into the realm of codes.

Codes matter in technical accounts concerning crime as they do in other sorts of technical accounts: because codes authorize their practitioners to carry on forms of investigation barred to nonspecialists; because codes actually govern the availability of relevant evidence; and because practitioners themselves fashion codes distinguishing between proper and improper procedures. In the case of crime, citizens have the right or even the obligation to report offenses, but on the whole only constituted authorities have the right to investigate, prosecute, and punish the same offenses. Existing codes generate much of the evidence available to specialists—for example, in published crime statistics. Finally, police, prosecutors, and researchers alike operate under rules that stringently channel their gathering, analysis, and reporting of evidence.

The NRC report concentrates on statistical systems. It recommends improvement in available statistical procedures by modifying and expanding:

1. counts and descriptions of violent events that are receiving considerable public attention but are poorly counted by existing measurement systems. These include but are not limited to intrafamily violence, personal victimizations in commercial and organizational robberies; violent bias crimes; and violent events in schools, jails, and prisons;

2. more comprehensive recording of sexual violence, including incidents involving intimates, incidents of homicide and wounding in which the sexual component may be masked, and more complete descriptions of recorded events;

3. baseline measurements of conditions and situations that are thought to affect the probability of a violent event (e.g., potentially relevant neurological disorders, arguments between intoxicated husbands and wives, drug transactions, employees handling cash at night in vulnerable locations);

4. information on the treatment of violence victims in emergency departments, hospitals, and long-term care facilities; links to data on precipitating violent events; and development of these data as a major measurement system;

5. information on long- and short-term psychological and financial consequences of violent victimization and links to data on violent events;

6. measurements of violence patterns and trends for small geographic and jurisdictional areas, as baselines for measuring preventive intervention effects; and

7. information system modifications to record more detailed attributes of violent events and their participants, in order to facilitate more

precise studies of risk factors for violence and evaluations of preventive interventions to reduce it. (Reiss and Roth 1993: 23–24)

These recommendations certainly reflect a demand for evidence
that would better reveal cause-effect connections in violent crime;
to that extent they seek to improve technical accounts of criminal
activity. Yet they center on calls for superior codes: clearer and more
comprehensive categories, more rigorous procedures for handling
evidence, and new rules of interpretation. As such, they threaten
conflicts with other established codes, notably rights of privacy.
Questions of appropriateness rather than of explanation arise precisely in this zone of code making. We begin to see how codes and
technical accounts, despite their starkly contrasting procedures for
generating reasons, sometimes complement each other. Codes often
reveal—or create—the empirical regularities that technical accounts explain.

Overall, nevertheless, the NRC panel was constructing a technical
account to reflect a current consensus among individually oriented
specialists in violent crime. Like their counterparts on many other
NRC panels, they were giving scientific weight to cause-effect accounts for phenomena about which public controversy had swirled.
They necessarily went beyond and challenged the simplifications of
stories about violent crime currently circulating in American news
reports, editorials, political speeches, activists' demands, religious
sermons, and existing public policies. They complicated matters by
insisting on multiple causation and by emphasizing causal relations
backed with research in credible behavioral and social science disciplines. To a world that often uses conventions, stories, or codes to
characterize violent behavior, they presented a technical account of
interpersonal violence.

Governing the Commons

Another NRC inquiry illustrates the distinctive character of technical accounts. In 1968, Santa Barbara biologist Garrett Hardin published a widely read article in the magazine *Science*, official publication of the American Association for the Advancement of Science. "The Tragedy of the Commons" recast Thomas Malthus's gloomy confrontation between limited resources and unlimited population growth. For Hardin, herdsmen with access to common grazing land illustrate the tragedy. Each individual herder gains an advantage from adding animals to the flock, since he gets more return from the whole flock but only takes on a small share of overcrowding's cost:

> Adding together the component partial utilities, the rational herdsman concludes that the only sensible course for him to pursue is to add another animal to his herd. And another; and another. . . . But this is the conclusion reached by each and every rational herdsman sharing a commons. Therein is the tragedy. Each man is locked into a system that compels him to increase his herd without limit—in a world that is limited. Ruin is the destination toward which all men rush, each pursuing his own best interest in a society that believes in the freedom of the commons. Freedom in a commons brings ruin to all. (Hardin 1968: 1244)

Contrary to optimism about the prospects for biotechnology and nuclear energy, Hardin identified the commons tragedy as a problem with no technical solution—no solution within the natural sciences alone. He voiced no faith in human altruism or prudent self-restraint. People would not automatically limit procreation with slowing expansion of the food supply, he declared, nor would increasing damage from pollution in itself induce polluters to stop. At the individual scale, neither enlightenment nor conscience would do the job. Hardin identified two possible solutions: privatizing the commons and "mutual coercion, mutually agreed upon by the majority of the people affected" (Hardin 1968: 1247).

Privatization of essential resources alone, Hardin pointed out, will not solve the problem. Distribution of a resource among current users as private property excludes from the former commons those who already lack use rights. Some commons—for example, water and air—resist privatization. Private property without coercion, concluded Hardin, would simply generate new tragedies of the commons. The choice simplified: mutual coercion or disaster.

Hardin's challenge started a whole new discipline: commons management. In an unusual collaboration between natural and social scientists, commons management enthusiasts studied overfishing, deforestation, water supply, population growth, and atmospheric pollution (Adams, Brockington, Dyson and Vira 2003, Dolšak and Ostrom 2003, Ostrom 1990, Pretty 2003). Beginning with critiques addressed to this feature or that of Hardin's analysis, the discipline's practitioners shifted toward two other enterprises: (1) studying human arrangements of shared resources that did not, in fact, escalate into ruin; and (2) creating new theories of conditions under which collective arrangements would succeed or fail. They discovered many instances of collective restraint in use of shared resources, and began to model how such instances worked.

Predictably, the NRC organized a panel on Common Property Resource Management bringing together the elite from this new discipline. In 2000, the panel's parent Committee on the Human Dimensions of Global Change, founded in 1989, decided to review work on the commons over the previous decade. As with the NRC study of interpersonal violence, the organizers commissioned a number of background papers, held a conference, and produced a volume, this one called *The Drama of the Commons* (Ostrom et al. 2002). But this time they did not wait for government agencies to ask for a study. They went out to the National Science Foundation and the Rockefeller Brothers Fund for the necessary money.

The scientists involved produced a technical account, or rather a series of technical accounts. The volume's editors implicitly distinguished what they were doing from conventions, codes, and stories by insisting on complex causation, including "indirect and mediated effects" (Ostrom et al. 2002: 457). Individual reports from group members took up irrigation systems, relevant psychological experiments, tradable permits, the impact of higher level institutions on local systems of resource management, the evolution of management arrangements, and a whole series of theoretical problems raised by the developing field. Valuable findings emerge, for example, from a simple recognition that pricing systems for irrigation water commonly fail without reliable storage (e.g., behind a dam) that makes possible an estimate of future supplies (Ostrom et al. 2002: 459).

By no means, however, did all participants agree; resource economist James Wilson complained that "nearly always, the literature on common-pool institutions assumes relatively complete (if stochastic) biological knowledge operating in a Newtonian world." At least in the field of fisheries, says Wilson, in defiance of these assumptions, cause-effect relationships exhibit enormous complexity, uncertainty about determinants of changes in the marine population therefore prevails, and uncertainty strongly affects the outcome of any managed intervention (Ostrom et al. 2002: 341).

Faced with uncertainty and with disagreement on detailed causal mechanisms, interactions, and sequences, the common-resource scientists made two interesting moves. First, for the human elements in their processes they mainly settled for simplified rationalist explanations of the phenomena at hand; their language highlighted incentives, costs, and benefits. As in the earlier NRC study of interpersonal violence, social processes entered the arguments not as direct causes but as precipitants or modifiers of individual decisions. Second, the scientists' strongest claims shifted from detailed causal sequences to favorable or unfavorable conditions for certain outcomes. Accordingly, the group's most general summary of the current scientific consensus ran like this:

> Effective commons governance is easier to achieve when (i) the resources and use of the resources by humans can be monitored, and the information can be verified and understood at relatively low cost (e.g., trees are easier to monitor than fish, and lakes are easier to monitor than rivers); (ii) rates of change in resources, resource-user populations, technology, and economic and social conditions are moderate; (iii) communities maintain frequent face-to-face communication and dense social networks—sometimes called social capital—that increase the potential for trust, allow people to express and see emotional reactions to distrust, and lower the cost of monitoring behavior and inducing rule compliance; (iv) outsiders can be excluded at relatively low cost from using the resources (new entrants add to the harvesting pressure and typically lack understanding of the rules); and (v) users support effective monitoring and rule enforcement. (Dietz, Ostrom and Stern 2003: 1908)

Here we learn about favorable conditions rather than detailed causes. Common-resource investigators are taking a frequent intermediate step in science: specifying empirical associations that hold over a wide variety of circumstances. The specification serves two purposes. It clarifies what investigators actually have to explain, and it sets logical limits on what could explain it. If these conditions apply widely, for instance, they make it unlikely that site-to-site variations in human intelligence, temperament, or regional cultures play the fundamental parts in success or failure of resource management systems. More likely, the crucial causes and effects involve interactions between organizational processes (e.g., connections and procedures in the fishing industry) and the dynamics of natural resources (e.g., the impact of depletion in the supply of one sort of fish on the undersea food chain). Adequate technical accounts will have to get those interactions right.

Codes and Competition

Once again, however, technical accounts articulate with codes. Measurement problems resembling those that arise in the study of crime also occur in studies of shared resources: who, for example, counts as a polluter or as a beneficiary in a cost-benefit analysis of pollution controls? But in current discussions of the commons, another sort of code looms larger: the code of property rights. Who owns what becomes a serious issue in common-pool regimes both because rights and exclusions strongly affect the viability of such regimes and because such rights and exclusions activate legal codes concerning public and private property.

When authorities issue tradable rights either to use a resource or to pollute it, for example, economists often argue that the rights should become secure private property so that users will have incentives to invest in them. Environmentalists, in contrast, "have argued just as consistently that the air, water, and fish belong to the people and, as a matter of ethics, they should not become private property. In this view, no end could justify the transfer of a community right into a private one" (Ostrom et al. 2002: 205). The debate between economists and environmentalists involves some cause-effect reasoning, but it shifts the ground to the categories, procedures, and interpretive rules of legal codes. Principles of equity and propriety take over from explanatory principles.

Although the NRC commons group reported considerable consensus within their own special field, they did not offer the only technical account of their subject available in contemporary science. In fact, another set of NAS-affiliated scientists were simultaneously pursuing related questions from the perspective of biodiversity, that is: "all hereditarily based variation at all levels of organization, from the genes within a single local population or species, to the species composing all or part of a local community, and finally to the communities themselves that compose the living parts of the multifarious ecosystems of the world" (Reaka-Kudla, Wilson, and Wilson 1997: 1). A number of specialists in biodiversity, drawn chiefly from evolutionary and ecological biology, dealt with their subject in quite different terms from common-pool adherents. They considered the documentation and maintenance of biodiversity as good in themselves, and typically advocated sustainable development: management of renewable resources so that world biodiversity ceased to decline under human impact, and perhaps even increased. Patrick Kangas, coordinator of the Natural Resources Management Program at the University of Maryland, College Park, identified these obstacles to sustainable development:

- overharvesting of renewable resources
- lack of markets for products from sustainably developed operations
- short-sighted political economies that do not properly value sustainability or the contributions of nature to economies
- land-tenure problems and the uneven distribution of land-holdings
- government subsidization of counterproductive land-use programs
- political backlash caused by the influence of developed countries on land-use and on conservation decisions of lesser-developed countries
- violent conflicts, especially over natural resources. (Reaka-Kudla, Wilson, and Wilson 1997: 394).

The list features social processes, but mostly quite different ones from the common-pool analysts. While the common-pool people concentrated on conditions for stable human cooperation, the biodiversity people stressed human interference—conscious or otherwise—in worldwide biological processes.

A later *Science* symposium on soil sciences illustrates the distinctiveness of the biodiversity perspective (Sugden, Stone, and Ash 2004). The symposium includes reports from specialists on soil degradation, melting of polar permafrost, the role of fungi in the viability of plant environments, soil carbon sequestration, human approaches to treatment of soil, ecological linkages between life above and below ground, and underground ecosystems. The presentations begin with a world map displaying erosion, pollution, desertification, and other human abuses of the soil, then proceed to an article on "Wounding Earth's Fragile Skin." Although notes of alarm at human ignorance, neglect, and destruction recur through the symposium, the main arguments depend on technical accounts emerging from biological research.

Codes reappear high on the agenda in the scientists' program. In this symposium, however, the crucial codes do not concern human behavior, but the measurement of underground processes:

> The representation of the diversity of microenvironments in soil depends on an ability to model the distribution of water, unsaturated solute flow, and diffusion in porous media. Techniques for some of these are relatively well advanced, but the modeling of multiphasic flow is still problematic. An integrated approach to studying soil with emphasis on the interactions between physical and biological processes is required to bring the science up to comparable levels with aboveground ecology. (Young and Crawford 2004: 1637)

Two groups of eminent scientists—common-pool specialists and biological ecologists—study overlapping phenomena. They propose competing definitions of what must be explained, competing explanations, and competing codes for evaluation of human intervention's effects. Their preferred technical accounts lead them in different directions.

Human Evolution's Technical Accounts

Technical accounts, we have seen, sometimes propose reasons for currently pressing problems and solutions to those problems. Often, however, they satisfy more general curiosity about puzzling conditions, origins, and destinations, the whys and wherefores of volcanoes, galaxies, population growth, or technical innovation. As evolutionary explanations of human origins and development have gained in richness and credibility, an old genre of technical account in this vein has acquired new popularity: the book providing evolutionary explanations of human prehistory and history for nonspecialists in the subject. In a nice phrase, the French call this sort of book *haute vulgarisation*, with *vulgaire* meaning not "impolite" but "accessible" to ordinary folks, and *haute* narrowing ordinary folks to reasonably well-educated readers.

Even for readers who are generally comfortable with evolutionary ideas, evolutionary explanations of human prehistory and history require skillful pathfinding. A successful author in this genre must somehow dispel the lurking thought that current differences in wealth or power between whole populations result from genetically transmitted capacities, manage controversies among specialists over such questions as whether natural selection occurs uniquely at the level of the gene or might also operate on individuals and populations, maintain the distinction between current scientific consensus and conjecture, yet balance the cause-effect account between complexity and uncertainty.

Let us compare three authors who have won the bet. Biologists Charles Pasternak, Luigi Luca Cavalli-Sforza, and Jared Diamond have all applied evolutionary ideas to humanity in widely accessible prose. All three have won their credentials in relevant hard science: Pasternak as a biochemist best known for his work on membranes, Cavalli-Sforza as a geneticist who shifted from bacteria to human populations, and Diamond as a student of bird evolution. All three find ways of simplifying the cause-effect accounts of genetics so that their readers need not become geneticists to follow the argument. Yet differences in what the three authors set out to explain introduce dramatic variations in how their accounts unfold. Pasternak focuses on what distinguishes humans from other animals, an inquiry that ironically but inevitably leads him to consider what humans share with all other organisms. Cavalli-Sforza proposes to explain the geographic distribution of genetic similarity and difference in the contemporary world. Diamond asks instead what accounts for marked variations in wealth and power among world regions, a question to which his answers finally reject human biological evolution as the crucial cause.

In order to bring out the distinctiveness of their technical accounts, let me sketch Pasternak's and Cavalli-Sforza's books briefly before dwelling at greater length on Diamond's explanatory strategy. Pasternak's *Quest* pursues dual objectives: to identify the unifying themes in all of biological evolution, and to connect human experience to those unifying themes. Quest, in Pasternak's view, characterizes all organisms from single-celled protozoa to humans. Quest ranges from quite passive to extremely active: from automatic movement toward light and food to willful exploration of the unknown. As Pasternak puts it at his book's very start: "As animals have become more highly developed over the past half billion years, so has their capacity to search. It has reached its peak in *Homo sapiens*. Not only do we search

for food and water, for a mate and for shelter, but we also search for
no apparent reason at all: it is curiosity alone, not need, that has led
men to seek the source of the Nile and to unravel the origin of the
stars" (Pasternak 2003: 1). As a complex book unfolds, Pasternak
complements this description with a technical account: successful
questing drives natural selection. From their emergence as a distinctive genus, humans have stood out from other animals. They have
inherited special physical equipment: "an upright gait, an agile hand,
the power of speech, a greater number of cortical neurons" (Pasternak 2003: 69). These combined to make *homo* the searching animal
par excellence.

Homo sapiens tops the pack, according to Pasternak, because of superior searching ability. Evidence of that ability appeared from early
on in massive migration, incessant invention, and ingenious adaptation to environmental change. In quest of these themes, Pasternak
divides his analysis into three main parts: the genetic basis of quest,
human quest with its consequences, and controversies over such
current quests as genetically modified foods. In each regard, he necessarily simplifies his cause-effect reasoning, not only providing
accessible cartoons of the causal mechanisms he employs but also
downplaying incremental, indirect, reciprocal, environmental, simultaneous, and feedback effects. As compared with the technical account of the same phenomena that Pasternak would offer to his fellow biochemists, he pushes the explanations of *Quest* toward stories.
Still, no one who hates or fears biochemical mechanisms should try
to follow Pasternak's argument.

The same holds for Cavalli-Sforza's *Genes, Peoples, and Languages*.
Although he proves himself superbly capable of taking the long view,
Cavalli-Sforza's own research concentrates on the medium term of
evolution: how mutations accumulate and produce change in specific
human populations over generations rather than millennia. He pio-

neered the reconstruction of human migrations and population inter-
changes by extrapolating backward from recent distributions of
DNA, languages, and cultural forms. In this book, however, he ranges
widely over evolutionary topics: an elementary introduction to genetic variation, a review of means for tracing evolution, applications
to the reconstruction of human origins and population movements,
diffusion of populations and/or agricultural technologies, historical
connections and variations among languages, cultural transmission
and evolution.

Cumulatively, Cavalli-Sforza shows that the perspective of population genetics illuminates far more than genetic shifts and distributions. He treads on delicate ground, since he argues simultaneously
that localized populations carry distinctive gene pools, that gene
pools are still evolving continuously, that physical environments have
durable effects on evolution's direction, that genetic inheritance affects susceptibility to environmental effects such as disease, and yet
that races do not exist in the conventional sense of the word.

Characteristics of the human surface, such as skin color and hair
type, do adapt, he points out, to climate; over the long term, for
example, equatorial populations generally acquired dark skins, while
polar populations developed light skins. When people could only observe variation in surface characteristics, they could more easily di-
vide the people of different regions into contrasting groups despite
the obvious presence of gradations in surface characteristics and the
crucial fact that all human populations could interbreed. Observers
could even imagine that skin color and hair type correlated closely
with cognitive capacity and other less visible characteristics.

Some less visible characteristics such as blood type (A, B, AB, or
O) do vary significantly in prevalence among major world popula-
tions; for instance, an estimated 98 percent of Native Americans have
Type O blood, while the figure for East Asia is 61 percent (Cavalli-

Sforza 2000: 15). But the work of Cavalli-Sforza and his fellow students of genetics establishes three facts of great importance for arguments concerning race: (1) little relationship between variation in surface characteristics and in other less visible features of genetic inheritance; (2) no well marked either/or genetic boundaries between populations; (3) on balance, great similarity in the genetic composition of all human populations. As compared with their closest relatives, the chimpanzees, all humans resemble each other greatly.

Many-Faceted Diamond

Comparisons of humans with chimpanzees often appear in popular presentations of evolution. Jared Diamond's Pulitzer-Prize winning *Guns, Germs, and Steel* follows up an earlier popular book, his *The Third Chimpanzee* (1992). As its title suggests, the earlier book builds on the great genetic similarity between humans and their two close relatives, chimpanzees and bonobos, or pygmy chimpanzees. The great overlap in genetic material and the large difference in historical experience means that small differences produced large differences. In particular, Diamond stresses genetically based human capacities for speech, cooperation and, paradoxically, destruction as differentiating the third chimpanzee from its kin.

The title of *Guns, Germs, and Steel* likewise broadcasts the book's problem: how and why did Eurasia, rather than Australia, the Pacific, or the Americas, come up first with the weapons, diseases, and metalworking technologies that subdued the rest of the world? Diamond cleverly makes the evolutionary perspective of his earlier book work against any sort of racism—any argument that people in different continents inherited different capacities to produce or contend with complexity. After three decades of field work in New Guinea, Diamond plays with the idea that as a result of dealing with less predictable and more demanding environments, New Guineans, on the average, have actually become smarter than Westerners (Diamond 1998: 20–21).

That argument, however, plays little part in the book as a whole. Diamond makes a quite different case. About 2,000,000 years ago, hominids who had already existed in Africa as distinct species for 5,000,000 years began to migrate out of Africa. Arching eastward along the Eurasian coast, by 1,000,000 BC they had reached Southeast Asia. In a later northward movement, by 500,000 BC, they had settled in Europe. Humans finally arrived in South America 12,000 or so years ago. By that time, humans—still a single species—had settled on all continents except Antarctica, and on many intercontinental islands as well. As of 11,000 BC, no notable differences in genetic inheritance or in social accomplishment distinguished the major areas of human settlement.

In a clever conceit, Diamond sketches how an observer at that point in time could plausibly have predicted that Africa, or the Americas, or Australia/New Guinea would make the Great Leap Forward that soon began. Over the next few millennia, dramatic differences did emerge among different parts of the world. But it was Eurasia that soon sped ahead in terms of technology and political power. By placing similar people in dramatically different environments, argues Diamond, nature performed a telling experiment. It endowed world areas with variable means of food production, and similarly competent people did the best they could with variable environments. Environments caused the differences among peoples.

Across the world, early domestication and diversification of food supplies produced advantages that then forwarded new innovations in technology and social organization, eventually favoring the development of superior weapons and metallurgy in Eurasia—in Asia before Europe, but soon across the vast continent of Eurasia as a whole.

What about germs? Diamond identifies an irony: the extensive Eurasian domestication of animals exposed Eurasians to a wider range of communicable diseases than other humans, the extensive circulation of populations within Eurasia spread the microbes causing those diseases, but it also built up resistance to them within the Eurasian population. Result: relative immunity within Eurasia, but killing epidemics when Eurasians reached out into other populations that had previously not been exposed to the killer microbes.

Diamond does not present this argument as an inexorable tale of triumph, stating his premises and then spelling out their historical consequences. On the contrary, he makes his technical account more dramatic by setting it up as a series of mysteries, establishing differences among major geographic regions before seeking explanations of those differences. Like students of violent crime who first identify differential crime rates, then try to explain the differentials, Diamond works from effects to causes. Indeed, he makes a classic distinction between proximate and ultimate causes. The proximate causes of Eurasian dominance, he declares, derived from Eurasian weapons, diseases, and metalworking, the "guns, germs, and steel" of his book title. The ultimate causes lay in differences between the Eurasian environment and those of other world areas.

The overall argument runs like this. Once we iron out the wrinkles, four main factors explain variation among continents. First, at the point when humans had reached all major world areas—Diamond's 11,000 BC—continents differed significantly in the wild plants and animals that were candidates for domestication, hence for organized food production. Australia, New Guinea, and the Americas, for example, lost most or all of their big mammals in late Pleistocene extinctions. Diffusion and migration within a continent then affected the spread of innovations in domestication from the few favorable homelands. That leads to the second factor: geographic facilitation of diffusion, which occurred more easily in the absence of major to-pological barriers and with east-west axes that reduced variation in climate, sunshine, and other conditions connected with latitude. Third, diffusion *among* continents differed, for example in the difference between the relative isolation of Australia, New Guinea, and the Americas, on one side, the proximity of Africa to Eurasia, on the other; most of Africa's domesticated livestock came from Eurasia. Finally, area and population size mattered because they intensified competition and multiplied points of innovation. Isolated islands lost out dramatically on the third and fourth counts.

Why, then, didn't sub-Saharan Africa lead the world? After all, its humans had something like five million years of advance on their neighbors. Diamond points to three main factors:

1. paucity of domesticable native animal and plant species
2. smaller area suitable for indigenous food production
3. a north-south axis, which because of differences in habitats impeded diffusion of food production and inventions

On this base, Diamond uses archaeology, linguistics, and genetic mapping to fashion a technical account of African history from 11,000 BC to the recent past. He traces, for example, the spread of Bantu-speaking farmers from a base in West Africa's inland savanna into broad areas of southern Africa, beginning around 3,000 BC. Throughout his book, Diamond overlays the broad explanation of regional differences with schematic histories. From my perspective as a European historian, of course, the story stops short just when it gets exciting: just *how* did those Eurasians convert their technical advantages into world domination? But Diamond certainly makes it difficult to allege broad racial or cultural differences as the fundamental causes of world inequality.

For Africa, Diamond sums up:

> In short, Europe's colonization of Africa had nothing to do with differences between European and African peoples themselves, as white racists assume. Rather, it was due to accidents of geography and biogeography—in particular, to the continents' different areas, axes, and suites of wild plant and animal species. That is, the different historical trajectories of Africa and Europe stem ultimately from differences in real estate. (Diamond 1998: 400–401)

The book's genius lies in connecting arguments at multiple levels of complexity: relatively simple arguments against racism and for geographical determinism; more complex arguments about human-environment interactions in different parts of the world, subtle (and often speculative) arguments about particular developments such as movements of Africa's Bantu populations. It qualifies doubly as a technical account; it both makes an earnest search for reliable cause-effect relationships and draws on a spectacular range of specialized knowledge. If we believe Diamond, it is not because his reasons for things are conventionally familiar, not because they conform to standard codes, not because they supply nicely simplified stories, but because we trust the way he draws on available specialized evidence to rule out some possible causes and enhance the plausibility of others.

Technical Accounts Revisited

Comparison of the evolution-based technical accounts offered us by Pasternak, Cavalli-Sforza, and Diamond identifies important similarities and differences. All three books (and many more like them) nudge their explanations far enough away from specialists' accounts of the same phenomena that, from the specialists' perspective, they look a lot like stories. From a general reader's perspective, however, they look much different from the everyday stories in which you and I package accounts of what has happened to us recently. We might call the best evolutionary accounts *superior stories*, since they adopt story form in their simplification of causal processes, but in general tell their stories by means of entities and cause-effect relationships corresponding to those appearing in defensible, full-fledged technical accounts. We learn again that the distance from stories to technical accounts runs along a continuum with cause and effect at both ends, but with agents and mechanisms drawn from a specialized form of causal analysis at the end containing technical accounts.

The Pasternak, Cavalli-Sforza, and Diamond books differ, however, in what they seek to explain. Pasternak focuses on similarities and differences between humans and other organisms, Cavalli-Sforza on the geography of human characteristics, Diamond on historic differences among continents in human technologies and activities. Nothing wrong with that; authors have the right to set their own problems, just as I have chosen to set up this book's questions in my own peculiar way. The differences matter, however, because they lead authors to draw on the same connected body of knowledge—in this case, evolutionary theory, broadly defined—in distinctly different ways. Pasternak shows us that a single unifying principle, which he calls "quest," helps explain a vast array of changes from single-celled organisms onward. Cavalli-Sforza spends much of his effort showing that the technical tools of population genetics produce surprising but coherent explanations for geographic distributions of human characteristics and activities.

Diamond, for his part, aims to demonstrate that human interactions with variable physical environments explain vast differences and changes in social arrangements. As he closes his book, indeed, Diamond holds out the hope that the same approach will also help answer such questions as why China has sometimes led the world, and sometimes lagged, in technological prowess (Diamond 1998: 411–17). At that point, to be sure, competing technical accounts from anthropology, economics, political science, and other disciplines begin to cry out for attention. That technical accounts offer valid representations of the disciplines on which they draw by no means guarantees their uncontestable truth. That depends on the truth of disciplines within their chosen areas of explanation, on the questions addressed by the authors of technical accounts, and on the fit between the two.

Inspired by Pasternak, Cavalli-Sforza, and Diamond, let this be our rule for superior stories: simplify the space in which your explanation operates, reduce the number of actions and actors, minimize references to incremental, indirect, reciprocal, simultaneous, environmental, and feedback effects. Restrict your account—especially your account of causal mechanisms—to elements having explicit, defensible equivalents within the specialized discipline on which you are drawing. Finally, remember your audience: you will have to tell your superior story differently depending on the knowledge and motivation your listeners will bring to it. Think of your superior-story-telling as relational work.

RECONCILING REASONS

Whatever else they do, governmental commissions give reasons. In the Anglo-American political tradition, royal commissions and their nonroyal counterparts regularly form by executive order during national crises. Like reports from the National Research Council, they broadcast consensus among authorities, and thus aim to still controversy. Composed of distinguished citizens whose reputations shield them from charges of partisanship and self-interest, commissions usually call witnesses and issue reports. But at the end, they offer their own considered collective judgment on the matter at hand— their reasons.

Lee Harvey Oswald assassinated President John F. Kennedy in Dallas, Texas, on November 22, 1963. The murder shocked the country, calling up a thousand stories about what and why. Kennedy's successor Lyndon Johnson appointed a commission headed by U.S. Supreme Court Chief Justice Earl Warren to report on the assassination. In the *New York Times* edition of the commission's report, journalist Harrison Salisbury described the tempest of conspiracy theories that sprang up around Kennedy's death. They resembled, he said, the theories that still circulate about the assassination of Abraham Lincoln. Small wonder, given the victim:

> Perhaps, because the tragedy occurred in our midst; perhaps, because so much of it took place before our very eyes on television, we have not fully realized its high drama. We have not grasped the fact that a blow which strikes down King, Emperor, Dictator or President has no equal on the human stage. When that blow takes the life of the mightiest

figure of the world none should be surprised if a shudder passes through society. Did not John Webster exclaim (in *The Duchess of Malfi*): "Other sins only speak; murder shrieks out!" (Salisbury 1964: xvii; having played in a college production one of the few characters in the *Duchess of Malfi* still alive at play's end, I savored Salisbury's reference.)

The Warren Commission concluded, and stated forcefully, that Oswald had acted alone, without coconspirators. Despite many contrary theories, the commission's findings hold up after forty years. Authoritative reason giving often works.

This closing chapter takes up three problems about authoritative reason giving that earlier chapters have raised but not resolved: what makes reasons credible, how people who work with specialized sorts of reason giving can make their reasons accessible to people outside their specialties, and what particular problems social scientists face when it comes to communicating their reasons, and reconciling them with the reasons that we as ordinary people give for our actions. Governmental commissions, we will see, offer just one of many ways to broadcast reasons. We will also see that the credibility of reasons always depends on the relation between speaker and audience, in part because giving of reasons always says something about the relation itself.

Four years after the Warren Commission reported its findings on John F. Kennedy's assassination, President Johnson appointed another commission. He charged the new commission with responding to the ghetto rebellions, rising violent crime rates, raucous demonstrations of the 1960s, and the 1968 assassinations of Martin Luther King and Robert F. Kennedy, as well as the widespread concern that America in general was becoming more violent. In his June 1968 executive order, Johnson asked the National Commission on the Causes and Prevention of Violence to report on:

1. The causes and prevention of lawless acts of violence in our society, including assassination, murder and assault;

2. The causes and prevention of disrespect for law and order, of disrespect for public officials, and of violent disruptions of public order by individuals and groups; and

3. Such other matters as the President may place before the Commission. (Eisenhower Commission 1969: v)

As commission chair, Johnson named Milton Eisenhower, brother of ex-president Dwight Eisenhower and former president of Penn State, Kansas State, and Johns Hopkins universities. The so-called Eisenhower Commission faced an even more daunting task than had the Warren Commission. It enlisted help from more than two hundred scholars in law, criminology, history, and the social sciences. I did my small bit by contributing an essay comparing American and European patterns of collective violence (Tilly 1969).

We scholars who participated counted it a victory that the commissioners did not adopt a stern law-and-order line. Instead, they recommended opening up opportunities for minorities and youth, giving young people more political voice, and using financial gains from ending the Vietnam War—in 1969, with peace talks just beginning, still a distant hope!—to increase American welfare benefits (Eisenhower Commission 1969: xix–xxx). They reasoned that inequality and stifled opportunity caused violence, individual and collective.

Commissions continue. On Monday March 31, 2003, the National Commission on Terrorist Attacks Upon the United States held its first public hearing at the Alexander Hamilton U.S. Customs House in Manhattan, New York, not far from the leveled site of the World Trade Center. At that hearing, commission members, Governor George Pataki of New York, Mayor Michael Bloomberg of New York City, the city's Police Commissioner Raymond Kelly, multiple survivors of the 9/11 attacks in New York and elsewhere, representatives of the victims, and academic experts on terrorism all testified. Testimony at the first hearing approached the vicious violence of September 11 from many different angles. When it came to giving reasons for 9/11, some witnesses offered conventions, some codes, some stories, some technical accounts, and some more than one kind of reason.

In the well-staged drama of commission hearings, we see very general processes unfolding. We watch participants not only giving and receiving reasons, but also negotiating their relations as they do so. The topics of terror and governmental responsibility raise the stakes of contests over reasons, and therefore allow us to see what happens when people care seriously about the consequences of giving one reason or another. But a closer look at debates over terrorist attacks and their prevention will finally show us that giving reasons about matters of life and death has much in common with the everyday activities of establishing, confirming, negotiating, and repairing social relations.

This book began with people seeking reasons for the devastating attacks of 9/11. Few of the first-round reason-givers, as we saw, offered technical accounts. At the time, most people who were immediately involved gave reasons in the form of stories, while others who stood at greater distances chose among stories, conventions, and codes. In their simplest versions, the three ran something like this:

STORY: Terrorists did it, but lax officials let them do it.

CONVENTION: Modern life is dangerous.

CODE: Because we have freedom to defend, we must combat terror.

It took longer for specialists to construct their technical accounts. Those accounts ranged across many different questions, especially how airplane crashes brought down supposedly unshakable buildings, what went wrong with American intelligence, why these particular attackers attacked and, more generally, why terrorist attacks occur at all.

Former New Jersey Governor Thomas Kean, commission chair, went round our full circle of reasons, invoking conventions, calling for adequate codes and technical accounts, but also telling stories of his own. Kean's conventions included insisting that the commission was nonpartisan (in fact it was bipartisan: five Democrats, five Republicans) and pointing out that the day's hearing would not adopt an investigative mode with the cross-examination of witnesses that would occur later in the commission's work. He called for organizational codes that would prevent repetitions of 9/11, which meant that the commission would have to examine the performances of government agencies with security responsibilities during al-Qaeda preparations for 9/11. He declared that the commission was consulting experts on national terrorism "to find out why things happened, how they could have happened, and what we can do to prevent their ever happening again" (9/11 Report 2003: 7). Thus he called for technical accounts, even if he didn't propose one of his own.

As for stories, Kean said this:

> Most of whom [*sic*] who died or were injured were Americans. The deceased and survivors were of all backgrounds, races, religions, creeds and even nationalities. They only had one thing in common. They were all at the time doing their best to keep ours, the finest, strongest, most productive, creative, diverse and welcoming democracy that has ever been created on the face of the earth, and, you see, that's what the terrorists sought to destroy.
>
> They wanted to extinguish the very freedom, vitality and diversity that characterizes the American way of life and makes it the bastion of hope for so many others in the world. (9/11 Report 2003: 4)

The public officials who spoke that day generally echoed Kean's giving of reasons for 9/11. Mostly, they told stories.

So did survivors who testified at the hearing. People asking the "Why?" of death, destruction, or disappearance often press for stories in which some person, entity, or force will bear moral responsibility for a devastating action. Indeed, the 9/11 commission came into being partly because of public pressure for stories. As the government slowly and reluctantly began inquiries into how it might have prevented 9/11, demands for convincing stories inevitably arose.

A group of New Jersey women widowed by the attack on the World Trade Center began pressing public officials for an inquiry. They got advice from veterans of the earlier campaign for an inquiry into the bombing of Pan American flight 103 over Lockerbie, Scotland, in 1988. And they played a major part in forcing the commission's public hearings on the government's own preparation—or lack of it—for terrorist attacks before 9/11. The women explained their involvement to a *New York Times* reporter:

> Three of them were married to men who worked for Cantor Fitzgerald, but the women were strangers until after the attacks. Ms. Breitweiser, 33, and Ms. Casazza, 43, voted for Mr. Bush in 2000. Ms. Van Auken, 49, and Ms. Kleinberg, 42, voted for Al Gore. All insist they had no political agenda, then or now.
>
> But they had a burning question. "We simply wanted to know why our husbands were killed," Ms. Breitweiser said, "why they went to work one day and didn't come back." (Stolberg 2004: 2; see also Dwyer 2004)

Clearly, for them an acceptable answer would not take the form, "terrorism happens." When Mindy Kleinberg testified before the 9/11 commission she had helped create, she made her position clear:

> Is it luck that aberrant stock trades were not monitored? Is it luck when 15 visas are awarded based on incomplete forms? Is it luck when Airline Security screenings allow hijackers to board planes with box cutters and

pepper spray? Is it luck when Emergency FAA and NORAD protocols are not followed? Is it luck when a national emergency is not reported to top government officials on a timely basis?

To me luck is something that happens once. When you have this repeated pattern of broken protocols, broken laws, broken communication, one cannot still call it luck.

If at some point we don't look to hold the individuals accountable for not doing their jobs properly then how can we ever expect terrorists not to get lucky again? (Kleinberg 2003: 6–7)

The question called for a story that would assign political and moral responsibility for the catastrophe. After the 9/11 commission issued its report in 2004, Kristen Breitweiser echoed Mindy Kleinberg's call. "Three thousand people were killed on 9/11," she complained in a September 2004 interview, "and no one has been held accountable" (Jehl and Lichtblau 2004: A18). By the presidential elections of November 2004, 9/11 survivors including the New Jersey widows had formed a pressure group called the Family Steering Committee that was publicly criticizing the Bush administration for failing to support the commission's recommendations (Shenon 2004: A20). Their story had gone political.

By the time the 9/11 commission was calling witnesses, accounts of survivors centered on terrorists who had willfully steered fuel-laden aircraft into the twin towers. Testifying before the 9/11 commission on the same day as Mindy Weinberg, Harry Waizer endorsed those reasons, but hinted that the U.S. government should have prepared for such eventualities. Waizer was a graduate of Brooklyn College and Fordham Law School who had worked for the Internal Revenue Service and then served in two New York law firms. At the time of the attack, he was vice president and tax counsel of Cantor Fitzgerald, with offices on the 104th floor of Tower One.

As he rode up to work about 8:45 AM on 9/11, somewhere between the 78th and 101st floors:

> The elevator was ascending when, suddenly, I felt it rocked by an explosion, and then felt it plummeting. Orange, streaming sparks were apparent through the gaps in the doors at the sides of the elevator as the elevator scraped the walls of the shaft. The elevator burst into flame. I began to beat at the flames, burning my hands, arms and legs in the process. The flames went out, but I was hit in the face and neck by a separate fireball that came through the gap in the side of the elevator doors. The elevator came to a stop on the 78th floor, the doors opened, and I jumped out. (Waizer 2003: 1)

Badly burned, Waizer walked down seventy-eight flights to ground level. An emergency worker met him somewhere around the fiftieth floor, led him the rest of the way, and found him an ambulance that took him to New York Presbyterian Hospital's burn center. Waizer fell into a coma that lasted six or seven weeks.

Still recovering eighteen months later, Waizer declared:

> I have no rage about what happened on 9/11, only a deep sadness for the many innocent, worthy lives lost and the loved ones who lost so much that day. There have always been madmen, perhaps there always will be. They must be stopped, but with the cold detachment reserved by a surgeon for removing a cancer. They are not worthy of my rage. Neither do I feel anger at those who arguably could have foreseen, and thereby prevented, the tragedies. If there were mistakes, they were the mistakes of complacency, a complacency in which we all shared. (Waizer 2003: 3)

By that time, the assessment of reasons was becoming clear: madmen struck the building that day, but our complacency made their strike possible. The story had become simple but compelling.

The experts, as expected, concentrated on accessible versions of technical accounts. Swedish-born Magnus Ranstorp, international relations lecturer at Scotland's St. Andrews University, testified later in the same hearing. He described himself as "a foreign scholar of militant Islamism and terrorism issues" (Ranstorp 2003: 1). In contrast to vivid reports at the same session from the violent attack's victims, rescue workers, and their survivors, Ranstorp applied sober expertise in Middle Eastern terrorism to the prevention of another 9/11.

With due simplification for a commission consisting not of specialists but of public figures, Ranstorp presented a technical account of terror. Like Jared Diamond's technical account of worldwide social evolution, Ranstorp's account of terror initially divided causes into proximate and longer-term. His proximate causes centered on the current organization and capabilities of al Qaeda and other terrorist networks. His longer-term causes consisted of changes at a global scale that facilitated terrorist activity:

> In many ways, 11 September symbolises the ultimate expression of the expansion of terrorism's global reach as an instance of what Mary Kaldor has termed "wild" globalisation. This "new terrorism" has harnessed the instruments of globalisation—the extension and improvement of cross-cultural communications and transportation; the continual migration of peoples—to transform itself into a multinational non-state enterprise, an infinite range of networks and constellations that stretches across the globe. Terrorist acts can now be controlled by remote-control from any distance or remote corner. The uniqueness of this new terrorism is that it has hijacked globalisation through riding the so-called techno-web, creating infinite new vistas of communication and attack modes, limited only by their imagination in the target acquisition and execution. (Ranstorp 2003: 2–3)

Later, Ranstorp enumerated a third, even more basic, level of causation: "root causes" of terrorism. They included unresolved ethnic and nationalist aspirations, poverty, and youth unemployment. But he focused his recommendations on ways of monitoring, blocking, and dismantling terrorist networks. He concentrated on countering the proximate and intermediate causes of terrorism.

Social scientists who built general technical accounts of terrorism divided their attention among the three levels of Ranstorp's analysis: proximate causes in the form of organization and tactics of terrorist networks; longer-term causes centered on the facilitation of terror as a political strategy; root causes such as generators of grievances and discontent.[1] My own small contributions to the public discussion concentrated on longer-term causes, but argued strenuously against the ideas that most people who employ terror resemble al Qaeda's conspirators and that most or all terrorist acts spring from the same causes (Tilly 2002b, 2003b, 2004b).

A Stern View of Terror

Rather than vetting my views of terror, however, we can learn more about reason giving by looking at someone else's analysis of terror. Harvard social science lecturer Jessica Stern wrote a vivid first-person "I-was-there" book called *Terror in the Name of God*. It does a superb job of making a technical account accessible to nonspecialists. Stern recounts how after years as an expert on terrorism—the Council on Foreign Relations gave her the resounding title Superterrorism Fellow—she began seeking out religious terrorists and asking them detailed questions about their lives. She looked for reasons in their self-conceptions. In her first round of analysis, she therefore jumped

[2] See, e.g., Futrell and Brents 2003; González Callejo 2002b; Kushner 2001; Pape 2003; Schmid 2001; Senechal de la Roche 2004; Smelser and Mitchell 2002a, 2002b; Turk 2004.

quickly from root causes (sources of personal availability and commitment) to proximate causes (strategies of terrorist organizations). As the book's dust jacket blurb by former CIA director John Deutch puts it: "All Americans now recognize the terrorist threat. Jessica Stern, a leading expert, adds much to our understanding in this readable book about the relationship between personal conviction and terror, providing a long look into the thinking of actual terrorists around the globe." Any valid technical account begins with well-stated questions. Stern identifies the two main questions she is asking clearly: (1) what grievances lead people to join and stick with holy-war organizations? (2) how do leaders run effective terrorist organizations? On her way to answers, she reports a fascinating pilgrimage through dangerous places.

What about grievances? Stern first interviewed terrorist Kerry Noble in 1998. Noble had by then served years in prison, convicted of conspiracy to possess unregistered weapons. During the early 1980s, he had risen to second in command of a militant Christian cult called the Covenant, the Sword, and the Arm of the Lord, the CSA. The CSA hoped to speed the Messiah's return to earth. They thought they could do so by overturning the United States government, which had sold itself to the Antichrist in the forms of Jews, blacks, the United Nations, and the International Monetary Fund. CSA members called their enemy the Zionist Occupied Government, or ZOG.

On the nineteenth of April 1985, federal and state agents laid siege to the weapon-packed 240-acre compound the cult had built in rural Arkansas. Three days later, after negotiations in which a widely known racist preacher mediated, the group's military Home Guard surrendered. Kerry Noble became a federal captive. Thirteen years later, Stern met ex-convict Noble and his wife Kay at their home in a Texas trailer park. By now Noble had become an anticult activist, but he had not lost his religious zeal. "Although I had been studying and working on terrorism for many years by that time," Stern reports, "none of what I had read or heard prepared me for that conversation, which was about faith at least as much as it was about violence" (Stern 2003: xiv).

Stern's interview with Noble started five years of travels across the world, seeking out and talking to Christian, Muslim, and Jewish militants who had committed themselves not merely to hate but to kill their enemies. Her subjects qualify as *terrorists* because they engage in terrorism, as she defines it: "an act or threat of violence against noncombatants with the objective of exacting revenge, intimidating, or otherwise influencing an audience" (Stern 2003: xx). They qualify as *religious* terrorists because they threaten or inflict violence, as Stern's book title puts it, in the name of God. They wage holy war.

What, then, are their grievances? Stern sees Jewish, Christian, and Muslim holy warriors as humiliated people who learn to blame specific others for their suffering. They seek to simplify and purify their own lives by participating in heroic acts that will simplify and purify the whole world. The humiliation may occur at an individual level, or it can result from stigma attached to a whole category of people, for instance all Muslims or all Jews. Since the world continues to reject the objects of humiliation and to persist in its corruption, the division between Us and Them becomes sharper and sharper. The division itself generates rage and a readiness to use any means, including lethal violence, against the enemy.

Kerry Noble, Stern reports, suffered from chronic bronchitis as a child. It so weakened him that in first grade he attended the girls' physical education class instead of exercising with the boys. Other boys bullied him. He wanted to be valedictorian of his high school class, but his family's frequent moves made him ineligible. The military turned him down because of his childhood illnesses. While he was working in an "awful job" after high school, one night he had a vision in which God gave him the gift of teaching and pastoring.

That vision started him on the long road to the CSA, along which he accepted the cult's division of the world into the few who would emerge sainted from Armageddon and the ungodly remainder condemned to awful, rapid death (Stern 2003: 22–24).

When she deals with individual terrorists, Stern's reasons come close to classic story form: circumscribed time and space, limited numbers of actors and actions, all causes located in the consciousness of the actors, tragic dénouements. However, when she gets to her second question—how leaders run effective terrorist organizations—Stern moves her technical account away from consciousness and toward interpersonal processes. What sorts of terrorist organizations survive and prosper, as Stern sees it? Stern singles out organizations whose leaders provide combinations of spiritual, emotional, and material rewards meeting the needs of people who are already seeking to participate in simplifying and purifying the world. Although charisma helps, steady provision of spiritual, emotional, and material benefits helps even more.

Stern observed terrorist organizations from close up. In 2000, she served as a defense expert witness in the trial of Khalfan Khamis Mohamed, a low-level al Qaeda operative who participated in the August 1998 bombing of the U.S. Embassy bombing in Dar es Salaam, Tanzania. Of Mohamed, she tells her standard story of a vulnerable youth who commits to a purifying cause. But soon she is relating the organizational process that drew him in, and shifting to the organizational structure of al Qaeda:

> Witnesses at the trial explained the structure of the organization in some detail. Bin Laden was known as the "emir," or leader. Directly under him was the Shura Council, which consisted of a dozen or so members. The Shura oversaw the committees. The military committee was responsible for training camps and for procurement of weapons. The Is-

lamic Study Committee issued fatwas and other religious rulings. The
Media Committee published the newspapers. The Travel Committee
was responsible for the procurement of both tickets and false-identity
papers and came under the purview of the Finance Committee. The
Finance Committee oversaw bin Laden's businesses. Al Qaeda had extensive dealings with charitable organizations. First, it used them to provide cover and for money laundering. Second, money donated to charitable organizations to provide humanitarian relief often ended up in Al
Qaeda's coffers. Finally, and perhaps most importantly, Al Qaeda provided an important social-welfare function. It was simultaneously a recipient of "charitable funds" and a provider of humanitarian relief, a
kind of terrorist United Way. (Stern 2003: 250)

Stern looked at many other organizations besides al Qaeda. She
recounts her conversation with Maqbool Pandit, who had held a
high position in the Kashmiri Muslim group called Hiz-ul Mujahi-
deen before he withdrew from activism. After answering a number
of questions about the group's operations, Pandit asked Stern about
her own views on the causes of militancy. "This fight," she reluctantly replied,

is about real estate, national identity, political power, and profits—both
personal and organizational. The fight is kept alive because organizations depend on it and because, on both sides, people are making a living. Smuggling goods. Selling arms. Lending money. Running camps.
Running "charities." Training vulnerable young men to believe that the
way to feel important and useful is by killing and getting killed in a
purported holy war. The jihadi leaders live in mansions, while their op-
eratives risk their lives. Agencies on both sides profit—professionally
and financially. Why would they want this "jihad" to end? I ask. (Stern
2003: 235)

Stern went on to say that humiliation, relative deprivation, and fear brought street-level militants into terrorism, but that the operation as a whole depended on support from rich sympathizers, sometimes including foreign governments. Pandit stayed silent for a long while, but finally agreed with her analysis (Stern 2003: 236). He was agreeing that political processes far from the individual grievances of ground-level religious terrorists explained the continuity and force of terrorist organizations.

Audiences and Superior Stories

If I had to bet, however, I would predict that people who quote Stern will favor the sections on terrorist psyches, and rarely mention what she has to say about political processes. The psychological section of her argument comes closest to the stories in which most of us package our explanations most of the time. It moves farthest from the technical accounts that social scientists propose for organizational processes. Aiming her book at an audience of educated readers and policymakers rather than her fellow political scientists, Stern makes her own implicit bet: superior stories will attract and educate her audience. The story of Kerry Noble draws us inexorably into her analysis.

Stern has adopted a powerful principle we have already seen at work in the treatment of technical accounts by authors and speakers who know how to reach nonspecialist audiences: instead of making specialists out of your audience members, translate your message into a form they will already grasp. "Superior" stories will often do the job.

Superior stories? Like everyday stories, superior stories simplify their causes and effects. They maintain unity of time and place, deal with a limited number of actors and actions, as they concentrate on how those actions cause other actions. They omit or minimize errors, unanticipated consequences, indirect effects, incremental effects, simultaneous effects, feedback effects, and environmental effects. But within their limited frames they *get the actors, actions, causes, and effects right*. By the standards of a relevant and credible technical account, they simplify radically, but everything they say is true. Superior stories make at least a portion of the truth accessible to nonspecialists.

As a classroom teacher, I make a strong distinction. My undergraduates come to class wanting to learn something about social processes. But most of them will become doctors, lawyers, engineers, entrepreneurs, business executives, or public officials. (Columbia University gets its pick of promising undergraduates.) For them, superior stories will work better and give them more value than would detailed technical accounts of the very same phenomena. They should learn how to recognize technical accounts and how to search for signs of their validity, but not necessarily to follow the cause-effect reasoning in technical accounts of social processes detail by detail.

If my teaching works, undergraduates will learn to read newspaper accounts of social processes more critically, to recognize interesting features of those social processes when they show up in their own lives, and perhaps even to support better-conceived public policies concerning those social processes when they have the choice. Solution: offer them just enough of relevant technical accounts and measurement codes to make them think about where the knowledge comes from and to intrigue the few future specialists among them. Otherwise, tell the liveliest superior stories I can manage.

Graduate students enjoy stories, too. But from me they get technical accounts and relevant codes most of the time. If successful, after all, they will do research that modifies available technical accounts and the codes that back up those accounts—codes concerning appropriate evidence, procedures, and reports of findings. Perhaps one of

my graduate students, for example, will come up with a better technical account of reason giving than my own, or a wonderful new way
of gathering evidence about reasons. Many of them will follow me
by telling future undergraduates superior stories. They can only do
so if they master the relevant technical accounts and their accompanying codes. That is why, from an outsider's point of view, my graduate students and I talk jargon.

Relationships between my students and me add up to only one
small case of a very large phenomenon: the giving and receiving of
reasons. But those relationships illustrate this book's two basic arguments. First, appropriate reason giving varies with the relation between giver and receiver; the point holds just as strongly for technical
accounts and stories as for conventions and codes. Second, the giving
of reasons creates, confirms, negotiates, or repairs relations between
the parties. Aristotle's analysis of rhetoric, after all, prepared us for
just such an observation. Conventions do much of everyday relational
work. We should be glad they do, since constant deployment of
codes, technical accounts, and stories would complicate life enormously without improving it. Yet stories are a great human invention,
since they provide a medium of explanation that is widely accessible,
flexible, and persuasive. When life does get complicated, stories take
over the bulk of relational work.

Reasons, then, interact intimately with relations. Let us revisit the
first chapter's conjectures on connections between reasons and relations, to see where they now stand:

*Within their own jurisdictions, professional givers promote and enforce
the priority of codes and technical accounts over conventions and stories.*
Lawyers, physicians, biologists, and social scientists have all shown
us this sort of claim to attention.

*In particular, professional givers generally become skilled at translating
conventions and stories into their preferred idioms, and at coaching other*

people to collaborate in that translation. We have seen this translation operating forcefully in medical diagnosis and criminal interrogation, among other places.

Hence the greater the professionalization of knowledge in any social setting, the greater the predominance of codes and technical accounts. Courtrooms, laboratories, and hospitals demonstrate the principle amply. We outsiders commonly experience that reliance on codes and technical accounts as jargon or mystification.

To the extent that relations between giver and receiver are distant and/ or giver occupies a superior rank, giver provides formulas rather than cause-effect accounts. Most dramatically, we have seen physicians handing down diagnoses and judges handing down legal decisions. The same principle applies, however, to priests, prophets, and princes.

Givers who offer formulas thereby claim superiority and/or distance. My frustrating encounter with Ragionier Ciampan in Milan when I wanted to photograph archival documents illustrates the principle. So does the discretion I enjoyed as a disbursing officer when a sailor asked for a payment and I got to decide whether the rules would let me give him the money.

Receivers ordinarily challenge such claims, when they do, by demanding cause-effect accounts. We have seen survivors of 9/11 making just such demands for accounting that will show who is responsible for their losses.

Those demands typically take the forms of expressing skepticism about the proposed formula and asking for detail on how and why Y actually occurred. Consider Mindy Kleinberg's vigorous rejection of "bad luck" as an explanation of failures to prevent 9/11.

In the case of authoritatively delivered codes, however, a skilled receiver can also challenge the reasons given by deploying the code and demonstrating that giver has misused it. Disputes over medical malpractice often center on this sort of exchange. Jailhouse lawyers—prisoners who have learned enough of the law to cause trouble—likewise follow the principle.

Even in the presence of distance and/or inequality, to the extent that receiver has visible power to affect giver's subsequent welfare, giver moves from formulas toward cause-effect accounts. Again, 9/11 survivors used political pressure and wide publicity to move the government toward an inquiry. In my academic business, the challenge runs, "Don't show me that you used the right statistics. Tell me how the phenomenon works."

These examples do not, of course, prove the principles. But at least they illustrate dramatically the relational side of reason giving.

Broadcasting Specialized Reasons

Still, the prevalence of conventions and stories presents a problem to specialists. People who draw their reasons from complex codes or technical accounts must choose between two alternatives: educating their audiences in the relevant bodies of thought or pushing their expositions toward popular discourse—toward conventions or stories, depending on whether the reasons involved concern propriety or cause-effect explanation. Physicians, lawyers, theologians, and other specialists who must deal regularly with members of the general public usually become skilled in converting codes and technical accounts into less forbidding forms of reason giving. I have already given my, well, reasons for preferring superior stories.

Of course, high authorities such as the U.S. Supreme Court or a group of Nobel-winning nuclear physicists can announce their findings and leave the conversion to other people. Despite intermittent challenges, most westerners have come to accept the claims of high courts and nuclear physicists to superior knowledge, at least within those specialists' domains. Some bodies of specialized knowledge, furthermore, have acquired enough prestige and urgency that schools teach students their codes and technical accounts. Although natural scientists and mathematicians deplore the general population's ignorance of their specialties, at least schools make an effort to teach students the fundamentals. Pity the linguists, anthropologists, and economists whose special forms of reason giving most students don't encounter unless they go to college!

Social scientists face a distinctive problem. As I can testify from years of personal experience, the social sciences carry on a complex courtship with stories, conventions, and codes. They claim to describe and explain the same social processes that nonspecialists habitually treat by means of conventions and stories. Hence a bundle of problems for social scientists: they are commonly proposing explanations of the very same behaviors and outcomes for which people learn early in life to give accounts in the modes of conventions, stories, and codes.

Social scientists' very evidence often consists of reasons that people give for their actions. Yet social scientific explanations frequently contradict conventions, widely available stories, and/or prevailing codes for actions. Worse yet, social scientists' proposed explanations often involve cause-effect accounts of why people give the reasons they do (Tilly 1999). As researchers, authors, teachers, and participants in public discussion, social scientists therefore find themselves causing offense and cultivating disbelief. In any case, they rarely reach general audiences with their technical accounts. When they do get through, it usually happens through one of three standard approaches: making visibly effective interventions in public life (for example, opinion polling); broadcasting the logic of social science (for example, newspaper columns on economics); or infiltrating public discussion by providing valuable catchwords or arguments (for example, the idea of the Lonely Crowd that David Riesman once made famous). But on the whole, social science's technical accounts stay within the academy, unheard by the general public.

Shouldn't social scientists simply emulate fields that have already found ways of communicating with lay audiences? After all, engineers, physicians, theologians, and other specialists who routinely seek their own explanations within technical accounts then often communicate with clients and lay people by reworking those accounts as stories. Converting technical accounts into stories makes it more likely that the listener will understand and accept the account.

But what if some social scientific technical accounts point to crucial cause-effect relations that don't lend themselves to storytelling, because they involve incremental, environmental, reciprocal, simultaneous, or indirect effects? No one can, for example, explain how international migration streams operate without paying attention to the subtle but powerful impact of previously existing interpersonal networks on who goes where and gets what job (Hoerder 2002, Tilly 2000). Most social processes involve similar complexities. Their explanation requires full-fledged technical accounts. But social scientists often have trouble making their accounts credible.

Might deliberate campaigns to disseminate plausible superior stories work? Social scientists have had somewhat more success at infiltrating available explanatory stories than at visible effective interventions or at broadcasting the logic of social science. Some of them have, for example, publicized the argument that if whole categories of people suffer systematic disadvantages, some combination of discrimination with distinctive life experiences—rather than, say, some crippling incapacity shared by all the category's members—accounts for those disadvantages. Here social scientists enter the arena as public intellectuals rather than as designers of pedagogy. Books, the mass media, and public forums provide the crucial opportunities.

In this version of reason giving, social scientists have little choice but to recast their technical accounts as readily recognizable stories. Such stories can never encompass all the relevant cause-effect relations. They can never incorporate the full range of incremental effects, environmental effects, indirect effects, reciprocal effects, feedback effects, and unanticipated consequences. Much less can they enumerate all of the professional's crucial specifications concerning initial conditions and contingencies. But at least superior stories can get right the cause-effect relations they do include. That in itself constitutes a valuable contribution.

In fact, almost every group of specialists faces its own version of the same problem: how to offer credible, comprehensible reports of findings, recommendations, and explanations it has arrived at by means of specialized codes and technical accounts. For their own work, for example, professional historians depend heavily on esoteric codes: proper use of archives, correct excavation and interpretation of archaeological material, appropriate analysis of art works, and so on (Gaddis 2002, Van de Mieroop 1999). They also construct technical accounts strongly embedded in recognized historical sources, previous research, and knowledge of the settings in which the events they are analyzing occurred. Yet when they turn to writing textbooks or publications for general readers, they have no choice but to suppress or simplify much of their professional expertise. Superior stories serve them very well.

The same goes for philosophers, theologians, cosmologists, biologists, physicians, lawyers, and generals. They must mix and match among four main alternatives:

1. speak only to fellow specialists
2. educate (some members of) their audiences in their specialized codes and technical accounts

3. recast their reason giving in the form of superior stories
4. count on translators and interpreters who already speak the language
   to do the recasting

Speaking only to your fellow specialists is the easiest. But it runs the risk that other people will misunderstand, misrepresent, or simply ignore whatever you are doing. Educating audiences in your specialty is a wonderful enterprise if you have the power and skill to do so. Depending on translators and interpreters—science writers, popularizers, and knowledgeable amateurs—saves plenty of grief when the translators and interpreters know their stuff. But for a wide range of specialists, writing your own superior stories has the virtue of making you think about the relevance of your daily work to humanity at large, or at least the humanity with which you make contact outside of your study, laboratory, or conference hall.

Even when it starts with technical accounts, reason giving doesn't end with writing and lecturing. Physicians and lawyers regularly have to translate their own technical accounts into stories their patients and clients can understand and act on. As they do so, they are establishing, confirming, negotiating, or repairing their relations with patients and clients. Remember physician Jay Katz's discussion of how to review possible treatments for breast cancer with a patient who has just received that chilling diagnosis: as compared with a surgeon who confidently rules out alternative treatments (and thereby claims a superior-inferior relation to the patient), Katz calls for careful comparison of the alternatives until the patient has enough information and confidence to make a choice. He is not exactly calling for physician and patient to become equals—professional knowledge of medicine still gives Dr. Katz access to ideas and information few patients possess—but he is describing a relation of mutual respect. The reasons we give shape our relations with the people who receive them.

We can also read this book's teachings in the opposite direction. The reasons people give you reflect their approaches to relations with you. Most of the time, conventions and stories confirm relations that you already knew existed: you instantly recognize the "wrong" convention or story, which claims a relationship you prefer not to acknowledge. When someone offers you codes or technical accounts in unfamiliar idioms, you rapidly choose between two interpretations: either this person has misunderstood the relationship between you, or she is claiming superiority and demanding deference by virtue of esoteric knowledge. If, of course, you have asked for a summary of the relevant codes and technical knowledge, you have already established the inequality of your relationship, at least for the purposes of this conversation. A clever, sympathetic interlocutor can shift the relational balance by pushing the account you have asked for toward conventions and stories. Giving reasons does a wide range of social work. That work always includes shaping the relationship between giver and receiver of reasons.

That is why, in fact, I have written this book as a superior story. Since you, I, and every other active human will continue giving and receiving reasons every day of our lives, we might as well understand how reasons work.

REFERENCES

Abbott, Andrew. 1988. *The System of Professions: An Essay on the Division of Expert Labor*. Chicago: University of Chicago Press.

Abbott, H. Porter. 2002. *The Cambridge Introduction to Narrative*. Cambridge: Cambridge University Press.

Abell, Peter. 2004. "Narrative Explanation: An Alternative to Variable-Centered Explanation?" *Annual Review of Sociology* 30: 287–310.

Adams, William M., Dan Brockington, Jane Dyson, and Bhaskar Vira. 2003. "Managing Tragedies: Understanding Conflict over Common Pool Resources." *Science* 302: 1915–16.

Adler, Bill, and Bill Adler Jr., eds., 2002. *The Quotable Giuliani: The Mayor of America in His Own Words*. New York: Pocket Books.

Atwood, Margaret. 1997. *Alias Grace*. New York: Anchor Books.

Barkan, Steven E., and Lynne L. Snowden. 2001. *Collective Violence*. Boston: Allyn and Bacon.

Bashi Bobb, Vilna. 2001. "Neither Ignorance nor Bliss: Race, Racism, and the West Indian Immigrant Experience." In Héctor R. Cordero-Guzmán, Robert C. Smith and Ramón Grosfoguel, eds., *Migration, Transnationalization, and Race in a Changing New York*. Philadelphia: Temple University Press.

Batcher, Robert T. 2004. "The Consequences of an Indo-Pakistani Nuclear War." *International Studies Review* 6: 135–62.

Becker, Howard S. 1998. *Tricks of the Trade: How to Think About Your Research While You're Doing It*. Chicago: University of Chicago Press.

Berger, Bennett M., ed. 1990. *Authors of Their Own Lives: Intellectual Autobiographies by Twenty American Sociologists*. Berkeley: University of California Press.

Bertaux, Daniel, and Catherine Delcroix. 2000. "Case Histories of Families and Social Processes. Enriching Sociology." In Prue Chamberlayne, Joanna Bornat, and Tom Wengraf, eds., *The Turn to Biographical Methods in Social Science: Comparative Issues and Examples*. London: Routledge.

Berwick, Donald M. 2003. "Errors Today and Errors Tomorrow." *New England Journal of Medicine* 348: 2570–72.

Besley, Timothy and Anne Case. 2003. "Political Institutions and Policy Choices: Evidence from the United States." *Journal of Economic Literature* 41: 7–73.

Bosk, Charles L. 1980. "Occupational Rituals in Patient Management." *New England Journal of Medicine* 303: 71–76.

Brill, Steven. 2003. *After: How America Confronted the September 12 Era*. New York: Simon and Schuster.

Bronson, Po. 2002. *What Should I Do with My Life?* New York: Random House.

Broyard, Anatole. 1992. *Intoxicated by My Illness, and Other Writings on Life and Death*. New York: Clarkson Potter.

Bruce, Robert V. 1993. "The Misfire of Civil War R&D." In John A. Lynn, ed., *Feeding Mars: Logistics in Western Warfare from the Middle Ages to the Present*. Boulder, Colo.: Westview.

Burguière, André, and Raymond Grew, eds. 2002. *The Construction of Minorities: Cases for Comparison Across Time and Around the World*. Ann Arbor: University of Michigan Press.

Burke, Kenneth. 1989. *On Symbols and Society*. Chicago: University of Chicago Press.

Burton, John R. and Jesse Roth. 1999. "A New Format for Grand Rounds." *New England Journal of Medicine* 340: 1516.

Burton, John W. 1997. *Violence Explained: The Sources of Conflict, Violence and Crime and Their Prevention*. Manchester: Manchester University Press.

Campbell, John L. 2004. *Institutional Change and Globalization*. Princeton: Princeton University Press.

Case, Christopher, and Ashok Balasubramanyam. 2002. "A Woman With Neck Pain and Blindness." *Medscape Diabetes and Endocrinology* 4, no. 1.

Catelli Case. 2003. "In the Matter of the Probate of the Last Will and Testament of Anna Villone Catelli." 361 N.J. Super. 478; 825 A.2d 1209; 2003 N.J. Super. LEXIS 235, from LexisNexis, April 21, 2004.

Cavalli-Sforza, Luigi Luca. 2000. *Genes, Peoples, and Languages.* New York: North Point Press.

CBS News. 2002. *What We Saw.* New York: Simon and Schuster.

Cicourel, Aaron V. 1984. "Diagnostic Reasoning in Medicine: The Role of Clinical Discourse and Comprehension." Unpublished paper, University of California, San Diego. 2002.

————*2002. Le raisonnement medical. Une approche socio-cognitive.* Paris: Editions du Seuil.

Cole, Steven A., and Julian Bird. 2000. *The Medical Interview: The Three-Function Approach.* St. Louis: Mosby (2d ed).

Der Spiegel. 2001. *Inside 9–11: What Really Happened.* New York: St. Martin's Press.

Diamond, Jared. 1992. *The Third Chimpanzee: The Evolution and Future of the Human Animal.* New York: HarperCollins.

————. 1998. *Guns, Germs, and Steel: The Fates of Human Societies.* New York: Norton.

Dietz, Thomas, Elinor Ostrom, and Paul C. Stern. 2003. "The Struggle to Govern the Commons." *Science* 302: 1907–12.

Dolšak, Nives, and Elinor Ostrom, eds. 2003. *The Commons in the New Millennium: Challenges and Adaptation.* Cambridge, Mass.: MIT Press.

Drew, Paul. 2003. "Precision and Exaggeration in Interaction." *American Sociological Review* 68: 917–38.

Duenes, Steve, Matthew Ericson, William McNulty, Brett Taylor, Hugh K. Truslow, and Archie Tse. 2004. "Threats and Responses: On the Ground and in the Air." *New York Times,* June 18, A16–17.

Dwyer, Jim. 2004. "Families Forced a Rare Look at Government Secrecy." *New York Times,* July 22, A18.

Eden, Lynn. 2004. *Whole World on Fire: Organizations, Knowledge, and Nuclear Weapons Devastation.* Ithaca: Cornell University Press.

Edgerton, Robert B. 1967. *The Cloak of Competence: Stigma in the Lives of the Mentally Retarded.* Berkeley: University of California Press.

Eisenhower Commission. 1969. *To Establish Justice, to Insure Domestic Tranquility: Final Report of the National Commission on the Causes and Prevention of Violence.* Washington, D.C.: U.S. Government Printing Office.

Falwell, Jerry. 1997. *Falwell: An Autobiography.* Lynchburg, Va.: Liberty House Publishers.

Feige, Edgar L. 1997. "Underground Activity and Institutional Change: Productive, Protective, and Predatory Behavior in Transition Economies." In
Joan M. Nelson, Charles Tilly, and Lee Walker, eds. *Transforming Post-Communist Political Economies*. Washington, D.C.: National Academy Press.

Fink, Mitchell, and Lois Mathias. 2002. *Never Forget: An Oral History of September 11, 2001*. New York: HarperCollins.

Fishkind, Russell J., Edward T. Kole, and M. Matthew Mannion. 2003.
"Minimize Undue Influence Claims Through Proper Drafting and Execu-
tion of the Will." *New Jersey Law Journal*, May 26, from LexisNexis, April
17, 2004.

Fitch, Kristine L. 1998. *Speaking Relationally: Culture, Communication, and
Interpersonal Connection*. New York: Guilford.

Franzosi, Roberto. 2004. *From Words to Numbers: A Journey in the Methodology
of Social Science*. Cambridge: Cambridge University Press.

Frazier, Ian. 2004. "Bags in Trees: A Retrospective." *New Yorker*, January
12: 60–65.

Futrell, Robert, and Barbara G. Brents. 2003. "Protest as Terrorism: The
Potential for Violent Anti-Nuclear Activism." *American Behavioral Scientist*
46: 745–65.

Gaddis, John Lewis. 2002. *The Landscape of History: How Historians Map the
Past*. Oxford: Oxford University Press.

GAO [United States General Accounting Office]. 2003. *Medical Malpractice
Insurance: Multiple Factors Have Contributed to Increased Premium Rates*.
Washington, D.C.: U.S. Government Printing Office.

Glanz, James. 2004. "Reliving 9/11, With Fire as Teacher." *New York Times*,
January 6 (Web edition).

Goffman, Erving. 1961. *Asylums: Essays on the Social Situation of Mental Patients and Other Inmates*. Garden City, N.Y.: Doubleday.

———. 1963. *Behavior in Public Places: Notes on the Social Organization of
Gatherings*. New York: Free Press.

———. 1971. *Relations in Public: Microstudies of the Public Order*. New York:
Basic Books.

———. 1974. *Frame Analysis: An Essay on the Organization of Experience*. New
York: Harper and Row.

———. 1981. *Forms of Talk*. Oxford: Blackwell.

González Callejo, Eduardo. 2002a. *La Violencia en la Política. Perspectivas teóricas sobre el empleo deliberado de la fuerza en los conflictos de poder.* Madrid: Consejo de Investigaciones Científicas.

———. 2002b. *El terrorismo en Europa.* Madrid: Arco/Libros.

Gould, Roger V. 2003. *Collision of Wills: How Ambiguity about Social Rank Breeds Conflict.* Chicago: University of Chicago Press.

Greenberg, Michael. 2004. "Freelance." *Times Literary Supplement,* December 10: 16.

Hardin, Garrett. 1968. "The Tragedy of the Commons." *Science* 162: 1243–48.

Hardin, Russell. 2002. "Street-Level Epistemology and Democratic Participation." Working Paper 2002/178, Instituto Juan March de Estudios e Investigaciones, Madrid.

Harding, Susan Friend. 2000. *The Book of Jerry Falwell: Fundamentalist Language and Politics.* Princeton: Princeton University Press.

Heitmeyer, Wilhelm and John Hagan, eds. 2003. *International Handbook of Violence Research.* Dordrecht: Kluwer.

Hershberg, Eric, and Kevin W. Moore, eds. 2002. *Critical Views of September 11: Analyses from Around the World.* New York: The New Press.

Hoerder, Dirk. 2002. *Cultures in Contact: World Migrations in the Second Millennium.* Durham: Duke University Press.

Horowitz, Irving Louis. 1977–1978. "Autobiography as the Presentation of Self for Social Immorality." *New Literary History* 9: 173–79.

———. 1990. *Daydreams and Nightmares: Reflections on a Harlem Childhood.* Jackson: University Press of Mississippi.

Insurance Information Institute. 2004. "Medical Malpractice." III Insurance Issues Update (Web edition).

Jackman, Mary R. 2002. "Violence in Social Life." *Annual Review of Sociology* 28: 387–415.

Jehl, Douglas, and Eric Lichtblau. 2004. "Review at C.I.A. and Justice Brings No 9/11 Punishment." *New York Times,* September 14, A18.

Katz, Jack. 1999. *How Emotions Work.* Chicago: University of Chicago Press.

Katz, James E., and Mark Aakhus. 2002. "Preface and acknowledgments." In James E. Katz and Mark Aaakhus, eds., *Perpetual Contact: Mobile Communication, Private Talk, Public Performance.* Cambridge: Cambridge University Press.

Katz, Jay. 2002. *The Silent World of Doctor and Patient*. Baltimore: Johns Hopkins University Press (rev. ed. [1984]).

Kitty, Alexandra. 2003. "Appeals to Authority in Journalism." *Critical Review* 15: 347–57.

Kleinberg, Mindy. 2003. "Statement of Mindy Kleinberg to the National Commission on Terrorist Attacks Upon the United States, March 31, 2003." www.9-11commission.gov/hearings/hearing1/witness_kleinberg.html, viewed November 10, 2003.

Kogut, Bruce. 1997. "Identity, Procedural Knowledge, and Institutions: Functional and Historical Explanations for Institutional Change." In Frieder Naschold, David Soskice, Bob Hancke, and Ulrich Jürgens, eds. *Ökonomische Leistungsfähigkeit und institutionelle Innovation. Das deutsche Produktions- und Politikregime im internationalen Wettbewerb*. Berlin: Sigma.

Krug, Etienne G. et al. 2002. *World Report on Violence and Health*. Geneva: World Health Organization.

Kushner, Harvey W., ed. 2001. "Terrorism in the 21st Century." *American Behavioral Scientist* 44, no. 6.

Lawcopedia ['Lectric Law Library Lawcopedia's Law and Medicine]. 2004. "Medical Malpractice." www.lectlaw.com/tmed.html (copied May 5, 2004).

Lieberman, Robert C. 2002. "Ideas, Institutions, and Political Order: Explaining Political Change." *American Political Science Review* 96: 697–712.

Lipton, Eric, and William K. Rashbaum. 2004. "Kerik Withdraws as Bush's Nominee for Security Post." *New York Times*, December 11, A1, A15.

Luker, Kristin. 1975. *Taking Chances: Abortion and the Decision Not to Contracept*. Berkeley: University of California Press.

March, James G., Martin Schulz, and Xueguang Zhou. 2000. *The Dynamics of Rules: Change in Written Organizational Codes*. Stanford: Stanford University Press.

Marjoribanks, Timothy, Mary-Jo Delvecchio Good, Ann G. Lawthers, and Lynn M. Peterson. 1996. "Physicians' Discourses on Malpractice and the Meaning of Medical Malpractice." *Journal of Health and Social Behavior* 37: 163–78.

Massey, Douglas S., Camille Z. Charles, Garvey F. Lundy, and Mary J. Fischer. 2003. *The Source of the River: The Social Origins of Freshmen at*

America's Selective Colleges and Universities. Princeton: Princeton University Press.

Maynard, Douglas W. 2003. *Bad News, Good News: Conversational Order in Everyday Talk and Clinical Settings.* Chicago: University of Chicago Press.

Mazower, Mark. 2002. "Violence and the State in the Twentieth Century." *American Historical Review* 107: 1158–78.

McAdam, Doug. 1988. *Freedom Summer.* New York: Oxford University Press.

McCord Case. 2002. "Evans v. St. Mary's Hospital of Brooklyn." *New York Law Journal,* July 19, from LexisNexis, May 5, 2004.

McKeon, Richard, ed. 1941. *The Basic Works of Aristotle.* New York: Random House.

Mills, C. Wright. 1963. *Power, Politics, and People: The Collected Essays of C. Wright Mills.* New York: Ballantine.

Morris, Aldon. 1984. *The Origin of the Civil Rights Movement: Black Communities Organizing for Change.* New York: Free Press.

Moss, Philip, and Chris Tilly. 2001. *Stories Employers Tell: Race, Skill, and Hiring in America.* New York: Russell Sage Foundation.

Murphy, Dean E. 2002. *September 11: An Oral History.* New York: Doubleday.

NAS. 2004. National Academy of Sciences website, www.nationalacademies .org/about/history.html.

New Jersey State Bar Association. 2003. "A resolution expressing the position of the New Jersey State Bar Association on medical malpractice reform." *New Jersey Law Journal,* May 19, from LexisNexis, April 30, 2004.

Newman, Katherine S. 1988. *Falling From Grace: Downward Mobility in the Age of Affluence.* Berkeley: University of California Press.

Nierengarten, Mary Beth. 2001. "Using Evidence-Based Medicine in Orthopaedic Clinical Practice: The Why, When, and How-To Approach." *Medscape Orthopaedics and Sports Medicine eJournal* 5, no. 1.

Niles Case. 2002. "In the Matter of the Trusts Created by Laura J. Niles." A-7/8 September Term 2002, Supreme Court of New Jersey, from Lexis Nexis, May 17, 2004.

Niles Foundation. 2002. "Laura J. Niles Foundation." www.ljniles.org.

9/11. 2003. National Commission on Terrorist Attacks Upon the United States, Public Hearing, Monday, March 31, 2003. www.9–11commission.gov/archive /hearing/9–11Commission_Hearing_2003–03–31.html, viewed July 12, 2004.

————. 2004. National Commission on Terrorist Attacks Upon the United States, *The 9/11 Commission Report*. New York: Norton.

Noonan, John T. Jr. 2002. *Persons and Masks of the Law: Cardozo, Holmes, Jefferson, and Wythe as Makers of the Masks*. Berkeley: University of California Press (2d. ed. [1976]).

Nora, Pierre, ed. 1987. *Essais d'égo-histoire*. Paris: Gallimard.

North, Douglass C. 1997. "Understanding Economic Change." In Joan M. Nelson, Charles Tilly, and Lee Walker, eds. *Transforming Post-Communist Political Economies*. Washington, D.C.: National Academy Press.

Ostrom, Elinor. 1990. *Governing the Commons: The Evolution of Institutions for Collective Action*. Cambridge: Cambridge University Press.

————. 1998. "A Behavioral Approach to the Rational Choice Theory of Collective Action." *American Political Science Review* 92: 1–22.

Ostrom, Elinor, Thomas Dietz, Nives Dolšak, Paul C. Stern, Suisan Stonich and Elke Weber, eds. 2002. *The Drama of the Commons*. Washington, D.C.: National Academy Press.

Pape, Robert A. 2003. "The Strategic Logic of Suicide Terrorism." *American Political Science Review* 97: 343–61.

Pasternak, Charles. 2003. *Quest: The Essence of Humanity*. New York: John Wiley.

Petroski, Henry. 1992. *To Engineer Is Human: The Role of Failure in Successful Design*. New York: Vintage. [1982].

Plummer, Ken. 2001. "The Call of Life Stories in Ethnographic Research." In Paul Atkinson, Amanda Coffey, Sara Delamont, John Lofland, and Lyn Lofland, eds. *Handbook of Ethnography*. London: Sage.

Polletta, Francesca. 1998a: " 'It Was Like a Fever . . . ': Spontaneity and Identity in Collective Action." *Social Problems* 45: 137–59.

————. 1998b. "Contending Stories: Narrative in Social Movements." *Qualitative Sociology* 21: 419–46.

————. 2002. *Freedom is an Endless Meeting: Democracy in American Social Movements*. Chicago: University of Chicago Press.

————. 2005. *It Was Like A Fever: Storytelling in Protest and Politics*. Chicago: University of Chicago Press.

Polletta, Francesca, and James M. Jasper. 2001. "Collective Identity and Social Movements." *Annual Review of Sociology* 27: 283–305.

Post, Peggy. 1997. *Emily Post's Etiquette*, 16th edition. New York: HarperCollins.

Pretty, Jules. 2003. "Social Capital and the Collective Management of Resources." *Science* 302: 1912–14.

Ranstorp, Magnus. 2003. "Statement of Magnus Ranstorp to the National Commission on Terrorist Attacks Upon the United States, March 31, 2003." www.9-11commission.gov/hearings/hearing1/witness_ranstorp.html.

Rashbaum, William K., and Jim Dwyer. 2004. "Citing Debacle Over Nomination, Kerik Quits Giuliani Partnership." *New York Times* December 23, A1, B10.

Reaka-Kudla, Marjorie L., Don E. Wilson, and Edward O. Wilson, eds. 1997. *BioDiversity II: Understanding and Protecting Our Biological Resources.* Washington, D.C.: Joseph Henry Press.

Reiss, Albert J. Jr., and Jeffrey A. Roth, eds. 1993. *Understanding and Preventing Violence.* Washington, D.C.: National Academy Press.

Richardson, Kristin M. 2002. "September 2002: Baylor Grand Rounds." *Medscape Diabetes and Endocrinology* 4 no. 2.

Riesman, David, Nathan Glazer, and Reuel Denney. 1950. *The Lonely Crowd: A Study of the Changing American Character.* New Haven: Yale University Press.

Riley, Matilda White, ed. 1988. *Sociological Lives.* Newbury Park, Calif.: Sage.

Roland, Alex. 1999. "Science, Technology, War, and the Military." In John Whiteclay Chambers II, ed. *The Oxford Companion to American Military History.* Oxford: Oxford University Press.

Rosenbaum, Thane. 2004. *The Myth of Moral Justice: Why Our Legal System Fails to Do What's Right.* New York: HarperCollins.

Roth, Julius A. 1972. "Some Contingencies of the Moral Evaluation and Control of Clientele: The Case of the Hospital Emergency Service." *American Journal of Sociology* 77: 839–56.

Rothman, David J. 1991. *Strangers at the Bedside: A History of How Law and Bioethics Transformed Medical Decision Making.* New York: Basic Books.

Salisbury, Harrison E. 1964. "An Introduction to the Warren Commission Report." In *Report of the Warren Commission on the Assassination of President Kennedy.* New York: New York Times.

Samuel, Raphael. 1981. *East End Underworld. 2: Chapters in the Life of Arthur Harding.* London: Routledge and Kegan Paul.

————. 1998. *Island Stories: Unravelling Britain*. Edited by Alison Light with Sally Alexander and Gareth Stedman Jones, London: Verso.

Schmid, Alex P., ed. 2001. *Countering Terrorism Through International Cooperation*. Milan: International Scientific and Professional Advisory Council of the United Nations Crime Prevention and Criminal Justice Programme.

Schwartz, Barry. 1975. *Queuing and Waiting: Studies in the Social Organization of Access and Delay*. Chicago: University of Chicago Press.

Scott, James C. 1990. *Domination and the Arts of Resistance: Hidden Transcripts*. New Haven: Yale University Press.

————. 1998. *Seeing Like a State: How Certain Schemes to Improve the Human Condition Have Failed*. New Haven: Yale University Press.

Scott, W. Richard. 1995. *Institutions and Organizations*. Thousand Oaks, Calif.: Sage.

Senechal de la Roche, Roberta, ed. 2004. "Theories of Terrorism: A Symposium." *Sociological Theory* 22: 1–105.

Shenon, Philip. 2004. "9/11 Families Group Rebukes Bush for Impasse on Overhaul." *New York Times* November 28, A20.

Smelser, Neil J. and Faith Mitchell. 2002a. *Terrorism: Perspectives from the Behavioral and Social Sciences*. Washington, D.C.: National Academies Press.

————. 2002b. *Discouraging Terrorism: Some Implications of 9/11*. Washington, D.C.: National Academies Press.

State. 2001a. U.S. Department of State. Office of the Coordinator for Counterterrorism, "Patterns of Global Terrorism 2000." www.usis.usemb .se/terror/rpt2000/index.html.

————. 2001b. U.S. Department of State. International Information Programs. "Powell: 'A Terrible, Terrible Tragedy Has Befallen My Nation.' " www.usinfo.state.gov/topical/pol/terror/01091105.html.

————. 2002. U.S. Department of State. Office of the Coordinator for Counterterrorism. "Patterns of Global Terrorism 2001." www.usis.usemb .se/terror/rpt2001/index.html.

Stern, Jessica. 2003. *Terror in the Name of God: Why Religious Militants Kill*. New York: HarperCollins.

Stinchcombe, Arthur L. 1997. "On the Virtues of the Old Institutionalism." *Annual Review of Sociology* 23: 1–18.

Stolberg, Sheryl Gay. 2004. "9/11 Widows Skillfully Applied the Power of a Question: Why?" *New York Times* (Web edition).

Sugden, Andrew, Richard Stone and Caroline Ash, eds. 2004. "Ecology in the Underworld." *Science* 304: 1613–37.

Swidler, Ann. 2001. *Talk of Love: How Culture Matters.* Chicago: University of Chicago Press.

Tetlock, Philip E., Jo L. Husbands, Robert Jervis, Paul C. Stern, and Charles Tilly, eds. 1989. *Behavior, Society, and Nuclear War: Volume I.* New York: Oxford University Press.

Tilly, Charles. 1969. "Collective Violence in European Perspective." In Hugh D. Graham and Ted R. Gurr, eds. *Violence in America: Volume I.* Washington, D.C.: U.S. Government Printing Office.

———. 1993. "Blanding In." *Sociological Forum* 8: 497–506.

———. 1995. "To Explain Political Processes." *American Journal of Sociology* 100: 1594–1610.

———. 1996. "Invisible Elbow." *Sociological Forum* 11: 589–601.

———. 1998. *Durable Inequality.* Berkeley: University of California Press.

———. 1999. "The Trouble with Stories." In Ronald Aminzade and Bernice Pescosolido, eds., *The Social Worlds of Higher Education: Handbook for Teaching in a New Century.* Thousand Oaks, Calif.: Pine Forge Press.

———. 2000. "Chain Migration and Opportunity Hoarding." In Janina W. Dacyl and Charles Westin, eds., *Governance of Cultural Diversity.* Stockholm: Centre for Research in International Migration and Ethnic Relations.

———. 2001. "Relational Origins of Inequality." *Anthropological Theory* 1: 355–72.

———. 2002a. "Event Catalogs as Theories." *Sociological Theory* 20: 248–54.

———. 2002b. "Violence, Terror, and Politics as Usual." *Boston Review* 27, nos. 3–4: 21–24.

———. 2003a. "Political Identities in Changing Polities." *Social Research* 70: 1301–15.

———. 2003b. *The Politics of Collective Violence.* Cambridge: Cambridge University Press.

———. 2004a. *Social Movements, 1768–2004.* Boulder, Colo.: Paradigm Press.

————. 2004b. "Terror, Terrorism, Terrorists." *Sociological Theory* 22: 5–13.

Tilly, Chris, and Charles Tilly. 1998. *Work Under Capitalism*. Boulder, Colo.: Westview.

Timmermans, Stefan, and Marc Berg. 1997. "Standardization in Action: Achieving Local Universality through Medical Protocols." *Social Studies of Science* 27: 273–305.

Turk, Austin T. 2004. "Sociology of Terrorism." *Annual Review of Sociology* 30: 271–86.

Van de Mieroop, Marc. 1999. *Cuneiform Texts and the Writing of History*. London: Routledge.

Waizer, Harry. 2003. "Statement of Harry Waizer to the National Commission on Terrorist Attacks Upon the United States, March 31, 2003." www.9–11commission.gov/hearings/hearing1/witness_waizer.html, viewed 11/10/03.

Weber, Linda R., and Allison I. Carter. 2003. *The Social Construction of Trust*. New York: Kluwer/Plenum.

Weinholtz, Donn, and Janine Edwards. 1992. *Teaching During Rounds: A Handbook for Attending Physicians and Residents*. Baltimore: Johns Hopkins University Press.

World Bank. 2002. *Building Institutions for Markets: World Development Report 2002*. Oxford: Oxford University Press.

Young, I. M., and J. W. Crawford. 2004. "Interactions and Self-Organization in the Soil-Microbe Complex." *Science*. 304: 1634–37.

Young, Robert Vaughn. 2001. "That Wilder Shore: Intoxicated with Anatole Broyard." www.phoenix5.org/essaysry (copied January 6, 2004).

Zelizer, Viviana A. 2005. *The Purchase of Intimacy*. Princeton: Princeton University Press.

INDEX

176–78; National Research Council reports from the, 129–30; sociologists, autobiography among, 81; technical accounts of terrorism by, 165–66
speaker-audience relationship: credibility of reasons dependent upon, 158; rhetoric, 72–76, 173; translation of technical accounts into more popular discourse, 95, 132, 171–73
specialized reasons: popular reasons vs., distribution of types of reason giving and, 19–20; problem of translating into popularly understood accounts (*see* translation across types of reasons and reason giving). *See also* codes; technical accounts
Der Spiegel, 12
St. Mary's Hospital (Brooklyn, New York), 115–16
Stanford University, 103–4
statistical information systems, 135–38
Stern, Jessica, 166–71
stories: biographies/autobiographies as, 79–84, 79–89; as a category of reason giving, 15–17, 19–23; codes and, gap between, 124–25; conjectures regarding, 173–74; converting into codes, 108, 119–23; examples of reason giving through, 61–64; excuses, apologies, and condemnations, 76–79; legal precedence of codes over, 101; 9/11 terrorist attacks, use in discussions of, 21, 160–64; rela-

tional work done by, 70–71, 93, 173; as rhetoric, 72–76; of sickness, 89–93; simplification of cause and effect in, 17, 64–65, 102, 171–72; social relations and, 16–17, 27–28, 30, 33, 95; superior, 155–56, 171–73, 177–80; technical accounts, distinguished from, 130–31; technical accounts, inclusion in, 169; translating to or from other types of reason giving (*see* translation across types of reasons and reason giving); variation in to match changing social situations and relationships, 68–69, 93–95; virtues of, 64–69; the work of, 69–72
street-level epistemology, 21
superior stories, 155–56, 171–73, 177–80
Swidler, Ann, 64

technical accounts: biographies in the form of, 80–81; as a category of reason giving, 15, 18–23; cause-effect reasoning in, 18–19, 102, 129–30, 134–35, 138; codes, precedence of in legal arena, 101; of commons management, 141–43; competing explanations of overlapping phenomena, 143–46, 155–56; conjectures regarding, 173–74; of criminal violence, 132–38; evolutionary explanations of humans and their history, variations in, 146–56; functions of, 130–32; for graduate students, 172–73; measurement problems leading to codes as complements